I AM ALBERTAN

A MODERN-DAY PHOTOGRAPHIC ESSAY OF THE ALBERTAN PEOPLE

TIM VAN HORN AND KRISTEN WAGNER

I AM ALBERTAN

A publication of:
THIS COUNTRY CANADA Ltd.
4617 46 Ave, Red Deer, AB T4N 3N2
www.iamalbertan.ca

The publisher gratefully acknowledges the support of the **Alberta Lottery Fund – Community Initiatives Program, Canadian Heritage** and **The Alberta Foundation for the Arts.**

Book design:
Combine Design & Communications Inc.

Cover concept + design:
This Country Canada Ltd. and
Combine Design & Communications Inc.

Editor:
Sandra Shields

Cover photographs:
Kristen Wagner & Tim Van Horn

Printed in Alberta on Canadian Paper by:
Sundog Printing Ltd.

Canadian Cataloguing in Publication Data
Wagner, Kristen, 1963 -
Van Horn, Tim, 1969 -
  I Am Albertan

ISBN 0-9738195-0-2

1. Alberta - Centennial.
2. Alberta - History - 1905-2005
I. Title.

I Am Albertan is dedicated to everyone – past, present and future – who has fueled the spirit of Alberta. This book honors the can-do initiative that characterizes the wild rose province and the hard work, on so many levels, that has built strong individuals, families, and communities.

Happy 100th birthday Alberta! Hats off to everyone who has given their all!

As a lasting legacy of Alberta's centennial, copies of this book have been placed in every school and library across the province – a total of 2,500 books – accessible to every Albertan in every community.

In making the Book Initiative possible, This Country Canada Ltd. was joined by the Alberta Lottery Fund-Community Initiatives Program, Canadian Heritage, as well as Sundog Printing Ltd., Enbridge Inc., Steeplejack Industrial Group Inc., Roxanne McCaig, Esprit Exploration Ltd. and the Ship & Anchor Pub.

FOREWORD

Archives & Photographs

Brock Silversides
Head – Media Commons; University of Toronto Libraries

As an archivist, I get exasperated hearing archives described as "dusty," "old" and "long lost." Most writers don't really know what archives are, so they tend to trot out the same hackneyed phrases. Unfortunately, there are archivists who also buy into this attitude, and are convinced that they are doing their jobs only if they are collecting material that is old or from creators who have already passed on.

I disagree heartily. Many archives do indeed contain old documents but they can be, and increasingly they are, contemporary bodies of work that are constantly being added to by their creators. Judgements can be made on their historical importance, even if they are not historical in the chronological sense. Describing something as being of historical importance does not necessarily imply that it is old – only that it is now, or at some point in the future will be, an important addition to the historical record.

Photographic archives are in a different league from other archives because photographs are more accessible, more engaging, more immediate. They can arouse emotions of happiness and sorrow, inspiration and anger. Depending on who is holding the camera, they can be considerably more accurate and believable than any written account. Individual images provide a snapshot of a person, place or event. An accumulation of photographic images from different viewpoints, different locations, and different times of the day or year can give an in-depth reflection and understanding of a region or a people.

Some of the best-known accumulative documentary projects that have passed the test of time include Edward Curtis's examination of the First Nations of North America at the beginning of the 20th century, and the Prairie Farm Rehabilitation Administration's recording of the effects of the great depression on rural America. Closer to home there is Orest Semchishen's thirty year documentation of the Ukrainian or Eastern Rite churches of Canada, George Webber's chronicling of the decline of the small prairie town, Lawrence Christmas's long term project photographing coal miners, and Steve Simon's sensitive documentation of the annual Lac St. Anne Pilgrimage.

Kristen Wagner and Tim Van Horn are heirs to this tradition. They save bits and pieces of their current physical and social environment by photographing the world around them, then assembling exhibitions or publications. For the past several years their environment has been Alberta, leading up to and during its centenary year. They approach their work with the outlook that what they capture with their lenses says something fundamental about Alberta attitudes, achievements and failures, and – most importantly – about everyday life. They have covered all facets of Alberta today: work, recreation, cultural activities, the natural environment, and the built environment. Their determination to keep this work together for posterity has resulted in this book.

There is a difference between reading history and writing history, and Kristen and Tim are writing history. Their work is neither dusty nor old; it is unique and important. Saved as a body of work, an archive in other words, this work will prove to be of increasing significance in years to come. Alberta should be grateful for the work that went into I Am an Albertan – trust me, future citizens of the province certainly will be.

INTRODUCTION

I Am Albertan

Sandra Shields
Author - Where Fire Speaks; The Company of Others

One hundred years ago, Ottawa drew a line down the middle of the North West Territories and created the provinces of Alberta and Saskatchewan. In a gala ceremony held in Edmonton on the first of September 1905, Alberta became slightly larger and three days older than its new neighbor.

I Am Albertan comes to you in the spirit of celebrating a century of life in the wild rose province. On the pages that follow you'll meet the people of Alberta: the small-town mechanic, the kids playing hockey on an outdoor rink, a family at the lake, a couple kissing on their wedding day, Mounted Policemen, office workers, oil rig roughnecks, a boy flying a kite on the prairie, and a girl in a cowboy hat leading a white horse.

Some of the faces are famous, but most of these photographs pay tribute to the lives that every one of us lead. They remind us that even as history unfolds on the public stage, it plays out just as surely in more common places.

For me, the history of this province came to life in a homestead in the foothills not far from the American border. On the beautiful fall day that Prime Minister Sir Wilfrid Laurier took the podium in Edmonton to deliver his Inauguration Day speech, my great-grandparents were homesteading in the shadow of the Rocky Mountains. They had immigrated from the United States in a covered wagon six years earlier and paid $10 for a quarter section of rolling prairie and a whole lot of hope. They were not alone. Starting in 1896, the Canadian government, intent on filling the prairies with settlers, had launched advertising campaigns promising cheap land in the last best west. Immigrants from across Europe and the United States, as well as some from central Canada, came to join the bands of First Nations newly confined to reserves, a few surviving fur traders, some former whiskey traders, the Mounties, and the ranchers and cowboys who had followed them.

As the territories filled up, the clamor for provincial status began. Westerners, regardless of where they had come from, didn't take kindly to being under the thumb of politicians over two thousand miles away. As a territory, the West lacked the power to collect taxes and instead got an annual stipend from Ottawa that was never enough to meet the need for more roads, schools and hospitals. The eastern politicians dithered, questioning whether the West was mature enough to manage its own affairs. By the time the prime minister arrived in Edmonton for the inauguration, checked into the brand new Alberta Hotel and rode the city's first elevator to his suite, the groundwork had been laid for an uneasy relationship between Alberta and Ottawa.

The new capital was full of rotting plank sidewalks, brothels and garbage. There was a housing shortage so bad that two years after the inauguration, 5,000 people were living in tents amid a typhoid epidemic. Edmonton had originally been called Edmonton House, a fur-trade post established on the North Saskatchewan in 1795, the main stopping point on routes north and west. Ottawa's Liberal government picked Edmonton to be the capital of the new province because the city was Liberal whereas Calgary, the upstart established as a fort by the North West Mounted Police in 1875, was Conservative.

My great-grandparents weren't in Edmonton for the inaugural celebrations. They were busy raising five of what would be their eleven children. Charlie, my great-grandfather, had borrowed money from a neighbor to buy a flock of sheep, then watched from under the brim of his black Stetson as a bad winter killed most of them. His wife Betsy grew a garden and kept chickens. Charlie, who did a bit of everything to make ends meet, was renowned locally for his sheep shearing and known by housewives for miles because of the Watkins products he sold door to door, nutmeg and vanilla and other household items, delivered through all sorts of weather in a horse-drawn wagon.

Ten years after the inauguration, Betsy had her second set of twins, my grandmother and her twin sister. The youngest two in their brood were brought into the world by a local midwife who was known for never having lost a baby. The family was still living on the homestead in the hills midway between the farming towns of Beazer and Leavitt. To the southwest, the horizon was dominated by a square-faced mountain called Old Chief that lay just across the border in Montana.

Grandma was born into a province that was in a flurry over prohibition. It was 1915 and the Women's Christian Temperance Union was allied with the United Farmers of Alberta and the Protestant churches in a campaign to ban what they believed to be the root of all evil. A referendum was called. Women didn't have the vote yet, so it was men who went to the polls and voted by 61 percent to close the bars and make selling alcohol illegal.

That was the same year that Nellie McClung and 200 women stormed into the Alberta legislature with a 12,000-name petition demanding women be given the vote. Farmers were becoming a force in Alberta politics and tended to favor women's suffrage. The popular Grain Growers' Guide wrote that farm wives, as partners in the hard work of living on the prairies, deserved political equality. In the next provincial election, not only did women vote, Louise McKinney ran for office and won the Claresholm riding, becoming the first woman to be elected to a legislature in the British Empire.

Having the vote didn't change the chores that needed doing as grandma grew up. Like pioneer girls across the province, she milked cows, fed chickens, picked and shelled peas, and helped her mother do the laundry. With her siblings she roamed the hills, gathered crocuses and shooting stars, helped with the annual gopher drowning in the spring, and went sleigh riding down the coulees in the winter. There wasn't much money, but there was always enough food; her mother's baked bread, a sheep her father had butchered, plenty of cream, butter and eggs. Neighbors would visit on Sundays and gather around the piano to sing.

Prohibition didn't last long. The province was full of hidden stills, every second Albertan was breaking the liquor laws, and bootlegging was estimated to be worth $7 million. In the Crowsnest Pass, where prohibition had never had much support among the Slovak, Italian and Welsh immigrants working in the coal mines, the biggest bootlegger was a folk hero who gave money to the poor and was elected as an alderman in Blairmore. When his son was shot at a police roadblock, the bootlegger and his son's girlfriend confronted a constable who died in the ensuing gunplay. The trial was a sensation with both accused being found guilty and hanged in May of 1923. Moderates began lobbying for the government to take the lucrative business of booze away from criminals and put the money in public coffers instead. The next referendum went against prohibition and the Alberta Liquor Control Board began its tight-fisted reign over the province's bars and liquor stores.

Grandma was in grade four at the Leavitt school several miles from the homestead by that time, walking back and forth through the long grass or riding a pony with three other kids. She was a good student and, by her own admission, often the teacher's pet and decided she wanted to be a teacher herself.

When she graduated, the Depression which had begun with the severe drought of 1930 was only getting worse. In some parts of southern Alberta, the CPR had to use snowplows to clear the 10-foot high drifts of topsoil covering the tracks. Money, as grandma would say, was scarce as hen's teeth. In 1933,

she borrowed $200 from a neighbor and went off to Calgary Normal School, an imposing building that is now part of the SAIT campus. She arrived in a city of bread lines; in Victoria Park the largest soup kitchen in the British Empire fed 2,000 people a day. For the eight months of training required to be a teacher, she shared a $15 apartment with another student, lived on oatmeal, and longed for the wide-open spaces of home.

Once her training was over, Grandma took a job in Leavitt at the same school she had attended as a child. Nervous and only nineteen, she was in the hallway on her first morning when the handsome dark-haired principal, a man ten years her senior, mistook her for a student and chided her for loitering.

The principal had grown up nearby. As a child, he loved animals and being outside and hated going to school. As a teenager, he and his best friend were wont to ride through town shooting off their pistols. In time, he heeded the advice his father had given him and got an education. By the time grandma met him, he was known to be an excellent teacher and an eligible bachelor, and though he was reluctant to get caught, he thought grandma had the right makings for a wife, so kept a close eye on her.

In politics, the Social Credit phenomenon was sweeping the province. Bible Bill Aberhart had been principal of a Calgary high school when his Sunday radio broadcasts gained him ears across Alberta. An Edmonton schoolteacher told him about the theory of social credit, and Aberhart

decided it would solve the hardships the Depression was creating. Liberally mixing social credit with Christianity, Aberhart took aim at the banks and big business, and watched as his following grew and grew. When his ideas were rejected by the ruling United Farmers of Alberta, Social Credit became a political party. The organizing started in January, Aberhart promised every citizen a dividend of $25 a month, and in August the Socreds pushed the UFA out of the legislature.

Grandma and her principal became involved in the campaigning when the principal's older brother, also a schoolteacher, decided to run on the Socred ticket in the federal election. He won and then won again, serving as a Member of Parliament for more than 20 years.

For Aberhart, victory turned into a long hard slog. Alberta had a massive debt, interest was eating up half of government revenues, and the province could barely afford to pay civil servants let alone give out dividends. As the Depression continued, Alberta defaulted on debt, and the federal government declared unconstitutional many of the new statutes designed to implement social credit. The Treasury Branches were one innovation that was allowed.

Grandma and her principal married in 1939 and a few years later welcomed their first child, a dark-haired daughter who would one day become my mother. Aberhart won another term with the ongoing support of farmers, small-town dwellers, and the urban lower middle class. The drought years of the Depression ended and World War II began, helping to get the Alberta

economy moving again. One of grandma's brothers went off to war and came back with a wooden leg.

In the middle of the war, Aberhart died suddenly, his health destroyed by volatile politics, and his protégé Ernest Manning took over. A Saskatchewan farm boy, Manning had been the first graduate of the Prophetic Bible Institute that Aberhart had started in Calgary years earlier. Only 34 when he became premier, Manning shifted Social Credit further to the right and worked at paying down the debt.

Alberta's financial situation was about to change. For more than ten years, Imperial Oil had been exploring in Alberta and Saskatchewan, drilling 133 wildcat wells that yielded nothing but natural gas. The company was trying one last hole in Leduc before pulling out of Western Canada. The head of the drilling crew, a preacher's son from Nanton, was known as Dryhole Turner because he'd been drilling nothing but dust for years. On the afternoon before Valentine's Day in 1947, Leduc #1 blew in and the province was on its way to wealth.

Back in southern Alberta, the principal had become assistant superintendent. He and Grandma had five children in all and raised them in a big house in the country that they built facing Old Chief Mountain. They saw their kids through scarlet fever, whooping cough, measles and mumps. The oldest ones still remember when the house was heated by coal and they used an outdoor privy. They were delighted when, in 1948, they got their first indoor toilet as a Mother's Day gift to grandma.

That was the same year that up near Edmonton, another well on the Leduc field came in as a gusher and blew wild for six months. Oil had been discovered in Turner Valley in 1914, but the Leduc field was ten times larger and would itself soon be overshadowed by fields discovered in the 1950s and 60s. Many of those oil companies were from the United States and as their staff moved north the complexion of Alberta became a bit more American. The money from oil and gas enabled Premier Manning to run the province like a corporation and, at the same time, provide some of the most generous social programs in Canada.

Rural electrification was one spin off of oil wealth. My mom was a schoolgirl when the government brought the convenience of electricity to their farm house. She graduated valedictorian of her class in 1959. A year later, her parents bought a television and the family began spending evenings with Ed Sullivan, Lawrence Welk and Hockey Night in Canada. The 1950s were a turning point for Alberta. At the beginning of the decade, the population was evenly split between city and country; by the end of the decade, 70 percent of Albertans were urban dwellers. Television had arrived, bringing Hollywood and the latest trends into homes like that of my grandparents. Cars were becoming more popular, changing the landscape of the province with gas stations, drive-up hamburger joints, and drive-in movie theatres.

My mother became a registered nurse and was courted by a young man whose father was a principal too, a friend of her father. They

married while the young man was finishing his studies in engineering, a field that was becoming a popular career path for Albertans.

By 1960, Alberta had passed the one million mark. Ernest Manning was still premier, a position he held for 25 years. His son Preston was just a child but he would inherit both his father's conservatism and love of politics. I was one of those kids born while Preston Manning's daddy was premier. My father had finished his engineering degree, done a graduate degree in business, and taken a position in Calgary with Mobil Oil when I was a few months old. It was 1966 and half the workers in the city owed their jobs to oil and gas.

When Manning resigned in 1968, Alberta was more secular than religious; no longer dirt poor, the province was well-off. By the time I started kindergarten, Edmonton and Calgary were among the fastest growing cities in North America and the Conservative party, led by a young lawyer named Peter Lougheed, was about to do to Social Credit what Aberhart had done to the United Farmers more than 30 years before.

Calgary had become a city of head offices. My sisters and I counted the construction cranes on new high rise towers from the back seat of the station wagon whenever we were downtown. On the few occasions when we got to visit our father's office, we loved riding up 29 floors to the hush of those carpeted halls and rooms with floor-to-ceiling windows.

Alberta was in sync with the growing consumer economy in the 1970s. As kids we looked forward to the family Christmas parties

thrown by whichever company our father was working for; we would be there in our best dresses and wait for Santa to call our names. There was always a lot of food; one year they brought in Macdonald's hamburgers and French fries and everyone got to take as many as they wanted.

While the government of Peter Lougheed was supporting an expanded petrochemical industry and investing in the oil sands, Alberta was waging a protracted battle with Ottawa over the control and pricing of oil. With the announcement of the National Energy Policy in 1980, Lougheed declared that Ottawa had marched into Alberta's house and occupied the living room. Albertans were outraged; Prime Minister Trudeau and the new Petro-Canada were unpopular to the point of hatred. Separatist rhetoric flared up.

By the time an agreement was reached that saw Ottawa leave Alberta's living room and take a seat on the porch instead, oil prices were about to drop. In 1981, world oil was $44, and by 1986 it had collapsed to $10. The boom had turned bust and the construction cranes in downtown Calgary disappeared. Layoffs began.

I remember the bumper stickers that said: "Please God, send me another boom, and I promise not to piss it all away this time." We were lucky, our father managed to get through the 80s without losing his job. We lived just outside the city and went to a country school but beyond having a big garden, our connection to Alberta's agricultural roots was more in the imagination than anywhere else. Some of our classmates still had fathers who farmed, though

they did so in air-conditioned tractors with stereo systems. We had cousins who rode broncs at rodeos, but we were more comfortable in shopping malls.

At university in the 1980s, one of my professors was Aritha Van Herk, a writer who wore a mink coat and was rumored to have bought a Porsche with the prize money she won for her first novel, Judith, a story about a secretary who moves to the country and becomes a pig farmer. In her class, we discovered that we didn't have to leave Alberta to find great writers. We read Joy Kogawa's account of the Japanese internment during World War II, fell in love with Sheila Watson's novel Double Hook and discovered Robert Kroetsch's Badlands, a gin-soaked odyssey along the Red Deer River in an old Mercedes.

After term ended, some of us met up with Van Herk in Drumheller one morning, piled into our cars and followed the white Porsche at high speeds down back roads, retracing the path of Kroetsch's protagonist. Somewhere south of Hanna, my friend and I realized we were almost out of gas. We stopped and the Porsche disappeared. Flat, dry-land wheat fields extended in every direction, nothing on the horizon. We had a map but couldn't decide which way was north. When we finally came to a farmstead, we talked the hired hand into selling us some purple gas. In the late afternoon, we got to Dinosaur Provincial Park, that ancient bone yard by the Saskatchewan border where we found Van Herk and our classmates drinking beer near a hoodoo.

Back in the 1880s, the first important dinosaur skull to be found along the Red Deer River was from an Albertasaurus, a fearsome dinosaur, a smaller version of T-rex, who got its name the same year Alberta became a province. The two tonne lizard ran around 100 million years ago; by then, the swamps that have become today's black gold were long gone, having preceded Albertasaurus, by 300 million years .

The rest of Canada sometimes accuses Alberta of being a bit of a dinosaur. We have a reputation as the redneck cousin of confederation, the member of the family most likely to hold politically incorrect opinions and voice them loudly. Of all Canadians, we're said to be the most American. In fact, many of us once were Americans; the early influx of American whiskey traders into the province was followed by American cowboys, American farmers, and finally American oil companies. It was an American who started the Calgary Stampede and helped make the myth of the West something of a secular gospel in Alberta. Although most of us live in cities, truck sales here are the highest in the country. Somewhere deep in our imaginations, we still live on the frontier even though the golden age of the cowboy was almost over when my great-grandparents arrived.

Since the time of the cowboy, Alberta's economy has been swinging from boom to bust and back again. The recession that began when I was at university in the 1980s was temporary too and with the help of the Winter Olympics, Alberta bounced back. Edmonton became home to the biggest mall in the world. Peter Pocklington sold Wayne Gretzky to the Los Angeles Kings. Former football player Don Getty became premier but a TV reporter turned Calgary mayor was waiting in the wings.

The millennium rolled over and Alberta history kept playing out. Ralph Klein's reign shows no sign of ending. Fort McMurray is the new boom town with oil reserves that are estimated to be the second largest in the world after Saudi Arabia. Albertans are some of the best educated workers on the continent and among Canadians are the most likely to have cell phones and internet access. Still there is something unvarnished about us, an eagerness to get into things that other people draw back from, be it a bar brawl or religion.

On New Years Day 2005, we celebrated my grandmother's 90th birthday. Four generations converged on a church hall in the southern foothills. The sun glinted off a layer of snow that had fallen through the night. The sky was brilliant blue. The air was snapping cold. In the parking lot, my cousin and I hugged, then stood and talked, pretending the weather wasn't biting. Inside, there were long tables loaded with food and almost a hundred people who are either descendents or married to descendents of the much-loved matriarch in the pink floral-print dress.

Born on a homestead, grandma grew up riding a horse to school. Ninety years later, she was cuddling great-grandchildren who live in subdivisions and ride in mini-vans. At the party, everyone wanted their photo taken with her, so sitting in a big armchair, she hugged one great-grandchild after another. As she faced the camera, history was alive in her smile while hope for the future shone in the eyes of the children she held.

I Am Albertan is a documentary made in the belief that history has a starring role for each of us. In the following pages you will find a record of today that is rich and personal, with echoes of the past and glimpses of the future, all captured in a panoramic account of Alberta on her 100th birthday.

In 2005, Alberta joins Johnny Boychuk in turning 100 years strong.

Born in Saskatchewan on June 16th, 1905, Johnny came to Alberta as a young man and worked as a stonemason on the Banff Springs Hotel before taking a job breaking horses. He bought a ranch, then enlisted with an artillery regiment for World War II. Back in Alberta after the war, Johnny opened the first riding stable in Canmore on his CrossZee Ranch in the benchlands below Mount Lady Macdonald; an area that Johnny says is his favorite place in the world.

Today, almost every trail enjoyed by hikers, bikers and horseback riders throughout the spectacular benchlands around Canmore was blazed by Johnny.

In this centennial year, I Am Albertan pays tribute to the people like Johnny who make this province tick.

Johnny Boychuk, Cross-Zee Ranch,
Canmore, June 28, 2004.

Copyright 1905   By G.D. Clark

Edmonton This very moment is The CAPITAL of ALBERTA A Province in Reality

Then...

Inauguration Day and swearing in of Lieutenant-Governor George Hedley Vicars Bulyea. "Edmonton, at this very moment is The Capital, and Alberta, A Province in Reality." Some of the participants included

Sir Wilfrid Laurier, Governor General Earl Grey, G.H.V. Bulyea (signing), Privy Clerk J.J. McGee and Lady Laurier. Edmonton, 12 noon, Friday, September 1, 1905. Photographer: G.D. Clark

Now...

"Ready, set, celebrate - one year to go!" With 100 Alberta Centennial flags and a backdrop of banners, Premier Ralph Klein and the

Also in attendance was the Honourable Lois E. Hole, CM, AOE,

Minister of Community Development announced some of the centennial plans for 2005.

Alberta's Lieutenant Governor; she passed away on January 6, 2005. Her grace, her generosity, her hugs and her smile will be remembered by all. Edmonton, 12 noon, Wednesday, Sept. 1, 2004.

Morley Beaver(Chief Walking Eagle) and Isiah Beaver with good sheep heads
at Kooteney Plains   1904

Then...

Stoney people,
Kootenay Plains, 1904.

Now...

First Nations Veteran at Lac La
Biche Powwow, July 2004.

Then...

Threshing on Kemmis Place.
Pincher Creek, circa 1904 - 1905

Hauling Grain to Vulcan, 1928,
Photographer: W.J. Oliver.

Now...

Bringing in the crop near Cluny,
September 2004.

Inland Terminal grain elevator,
Legacy Junction, August 2004.

Then...

Construction of the Calgary
Milling Company mill, Calgary,
circa 1898 - 1899.

Now...

Elevator demolition in
Bashaw, 1999.

Then...

First oil well in Western Canada at Oil City near Waterton Lakes, circa 1905. Drilling began in 1901 and oil was struck in 1902 at a depth of 1024 feet. The well failed to maintain its initial flow of 300 barrels per day and by 1904 production had dwindled to almost nothing. Further exploitations in the Waterton area proved fruitless, but the brief success of the well encouraged a widespread search, which led to the discovery of the Turner Valley field in 1914.

Construction of Canadian Pacific Railway High Level Bridge, the longest trestle bridge in the world, Lethbridge, circa 1901-1908.

Curtiss-type biplane, the "West Wind" at Calgary in 1913. Photographer: W.J. Oliver.

Now...

Crossfield gas plant, September 2004. The province accounts for 55 percent of Canada's conventional crude oil, 80 percent of its natural gas, more than 90 percent of its liquefied petroleum gases, 49 percent of its coal, and 100 percent of its bitumen and synthetic crude oil.

Track Maintenance Crew, High Level Bridge (still the longest trestle bridge in the world), Lethbridge, September 2004.

Pilot for Air Mikisew, Fort McMurray, August 2004.

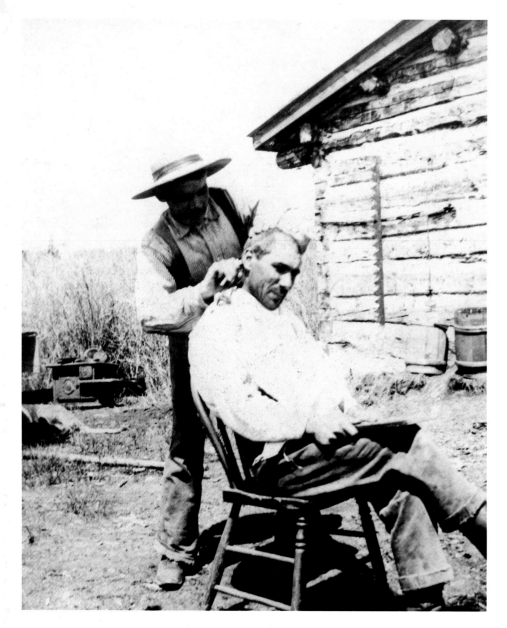

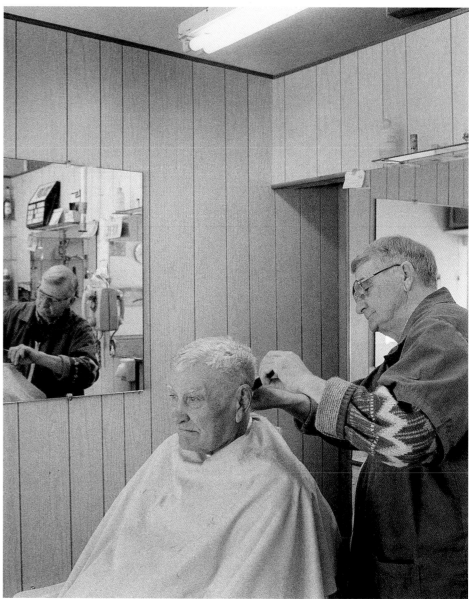

Then...

Man receiving haircut,
Dogpound area, circa 1905.

Pincher Creek Fire Brigade, Pincher
Creek, circa 1906 - 1907.

Now...

Neil the Barber, Red Deer,
May 2003.

Firefighters and Emergency
Medical Services (EMS) graduating
class, Vermillion, 2004.

Then...

Constable Fred Moses and friend, Royal North-West Mounted Policemen, circa 1906.

Now...

Calgary Police Officers, Constable Lak Johal and Constable Clark Budd, at work during the infamous Labour Day Football Game in Calgary; an annual tradition pitting the Calgary Stampeders against long-time rivals, the Edmonton Eskimos.

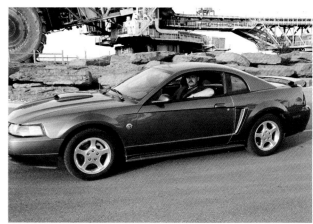

Then...

Hull's Terrace, Calgary,
circa 1900-1903.

First automobile – a Ford –
in Medicine Hat, 1905.

Mr. and Mrs. Joseph Descheneau,
Camrose, circa 1905.

Now...

A new house for sale west of
Calgary, August 2004.

2004 Ford Mustang, Fort
McMurray, August 2004.

A couple have a moment together
along the Elbow River, Calgary,
August 2004.

Then...

Baseball team, Canmore, 1905.
Photographer: Trueman.

Percy and Marjorie Copithorne
with fish from Jumping Pound,
circa 1904-1905.

Now...

The Grouard 86ers travel to ball
tournaments across Alberta;
McLennan, 2004

Kids at Kakut Lake with their catch,
August, 2004.

Then...

Interior of Asp Brothers store,
Wetaskiwin, 1905.

Now...

Interior of IGA store, Rocky
Mountain House, 2004.

Then...

Destitute family in Edmonton, while returning to Saskatoon from the Peace River country, June 28, 1934. Photographer: McDermid Studio.

Now...

Lynda, Ron and son Michael Pierzchala, from Lethbridge, enjoy their third season traveling from event to event in the summer months serving up some very fine fries. Here they are at the 13th annual Pincher Creek Kite Festival, near Old Man Dam, July 18, 2004.

Alberta Faces

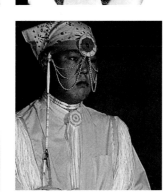

1

2

1 Rock pile, Blackfalds.

2 Grain farmers, near Crossfield.

3 Mr. Fred Winters at his Century farm near Millet. The farm has been in the Winters' name for over one hundred years.

4 Calf show and auction, Vulcan.

5 Bassano Dam irrigates southern Alberta's dry lands, Bassano.

6 (opposite page) The Jensens, from left, Derek, Darcy, Daron and papa David could not farm without irrigation. Kent Bullock, right, is the district engineer for the Taber Irrigation District. They stand before their fine August corn crop. One of David's four sons was absent on photo day, near Taber.

7 (next spread) Testing at the Beaverlodge Research Farm, Beaverlodge.

3

4

5

→ By 1910, Alberta settlers had cultivated 3.3 million acres of land by pulling stumps, clearing bush and trees, picking countless rocks and sometimes even pulling the plow themselves.

→ Agriculture and food production is the largest industry in Alberta and impacts one out of every three jobs in the province. Alberta is the second largest agricultural producer in Canada. There are 53,000 farms in Alberta that account for 23 percent of national farm cash receipts generated from primary agriculture.

→ More than thirty percent of Alberta's land is used for crops and livestock.

→ There are almost twice as many beef cattle in the province as there are people.

→ While only five percent of Alberta's farmed land is irrigated, it produces close to 20 percent of the province's agricultural yield. Today's 1.5 million acres of irrigated crops include potatoes, sugar beets, corn, peas, beans and mint, as well as many forage, cereal and oil seed crops.

Sixty percent of Canada's total irrigated land is in Alberta. There are more than 7,500 kilometres of irrigation canals in Alberta.

→ Irrigation has been practiced in Alberta for over 100 years and has transformed the prairies from the Rocky Mountains to Saskatchewan. In regions where there was once virtually no naturally standing water, canals, reservoirs and drains carry the life blood of water.

1

2

1   Beekeeprs, Theisen.

2   A ranch hand rounds up cattle
     near Black Diamond.

3   The first llama Tony Fiedler
     bought was mean and ugly and
     named Chretien. That was in 1993.
     He was happy to sell Chretien and
     buy a pregnant female at a sale for
     $10,000. Today he has between
     80 and 100 llamas and has a name
     for each one of them, Whirlwind
     Llama Co. Ltd., Barnwell.

4   Farmer loading producer cars,
     Sexsmith.

5   Three Hills Hutterite Colony, a
     brand new colony begun in 2004,
     farms on 5,500 acres near
     Three Hills.

6   The Haupt family grows
     sunflowers near Seven Persons.

3

4

→ Since 1915, The Beaverlodge Research Farm has conducted research into improved production crop, honey bee and pollinating systems adapted to environmental conditions in northwestern Canada. The farm has also developed appropriate technology for managing the resources of the region to ensure a productive and sustainable agricultural industry. The farm is part of the Lacombe Research Centre which was established in 1907 to serve central and northern Alberta and northeastern British Columbia.

→ Bees have been producing honey the same way they do today for at least 150 million years.

To make one pound of honey, bees must tap two million flowers and fly over 88,514 kms. A honey bee flies at about 24 kms per hour and in her lifetime an average worker bee will make 1/12th of a teaspoon of honey. Bees stroke their wings 11,400 times per minute, making their distinctive buzz. They communicate with one another by dancing in a way that alerts other bees and tells them where nectar and pollen is located. The dance explains direction and distance.

There are more than 200,000 colonies of honey bees in Alberta.

→ Alberta leads the country in honey production with 35 percent of Canada's production. When you see a bee on a flower, that's good news for honey lovers. The bee takes the nectar from the flower and makes honey from it. But the same bee is also doing a good turn for Alberta's crop. The link between honey production

5

6

and healthy crops deserves to be better understood.

"We estimate that for every dollar's worth of honey production, Alberta bees create $3 worth of value in the field." – Alberta Honey Producers' Co-operative

→ Llamas are bred and grown for their hair (fibre), as pack animals, for breeding and for meat. There are four llama species – the llamas, alpacas, guanacos and vicuna. Llamas were re-introduced to North America around 1870 through zoos and private game

farms. In 1930 there were approximately 400 llamas and guanacos. Today the number of registered animals is 147,000 llamas and 35,000 alpacas.

→ In 2003, Alberta harvested more than 6,000 acres of wheat.
→ Almost 16,000 Alberta farmers grow wheat; 36 grow sunflowers.

The sunflower is considered a new world crop as it was introduced to the early Europeans when they

came to America and found Native Indians cultivating sunflowers from Canada to Mexico and from the mouth of the Columbia River to the east coast.

→ Beef is the province's number one agricultural commodity. Almost 60 percent of Canada's beef is produced in Alberta.

1 Corinza the sheep is sheered by specialist Don Wytinck, Calgary Stampede.

2 A farming operation with 800 sows near Cluny.

3 Spraying crops, near Ribstone.

4 (opposite page) "Time goes by pretty quickly," says a retired farmer near Lessard. Together with his son he manages 64 sections of mostly cattle with some grain for feed.

5 (next spread) Sorting potatoes for potato chip production, Duchess.

→ There are just over 2 million pigs in Alberta on 2,677 farms. Pork makes up 40 percent of the total meat production in Canada and hog production brings in more than $3 billion to the country's economy.

→ There are approximately 2,500 Alberta sheep producers and 171,000 sheep in the province.

First introduced over 100 years ago, Alberta's early flocks were raised on the range and were selected for their adaptability to Alberta's varying climate.

The main sheep by-products today are meat, they are used in genetic study and to a lesser extent, wool.

The border closure that began in 2003 as a result of BSE cases in Alberta also includes sheep.

→ Potato chips were created by accident in 1853 in Saratoga Springs, N.Y. when railroad magnate Commodore Cornelius Vanderbilt complained that his potatoes were cut too thick. Angered, Chef George

Crum sliced some potatoes paper thin, fried them in hot oil, salted, and served them just to spite his fussy guest. To everyone's surprise, Vanderbilt loved his "Saratoga Crunch Chips."

1   Cattle drive in Longview area.

2   Stockyard conversation, Killam.

3   Calf show and auction, Vulcan.

4   The grip of the BSE crisis got this gas station in Seven Persons.

5   Farmer rally supporting farmers during the BSE border closures, Ponoka.

6   (next spread / left) Butcher with side of bison, Manning.

7   (next spread / right) Grass seed packager and salesman, Clairmont. Grass seed is purchased from across the province and Wal-Mart is their biggest customer.

> **BSE: What happened?**
In May of 2003, Alberta confirmed a case of mad cow disease. The United States, Japan, South Korea, Australia and other countries imposed temporary bans on Canadian beef. About 42 percent of Canada's beef cattle were in Alberta at the time. Alberta's share of total beef exports was 39 percent which was worth about $860 million a year. Ranchers were hit hard.

In the summer of 2003, the U.S. border reopened to some Canadian beef, but not to live cattle and, in Alberta, a cow that would have sold for $1,300 was selling for $15. Barbeques were held to promote Alberta beef and some ranchers began selling their beef direct to the public from refrigerator trucks and roadside stands.

The border remained closed to live cattle throughout 2004. In December, when President Bush visited Canada and dined on Alberta beef, he said the American border would open to live cattle within a few months. Two other cases of mad cow disease were discovered soon after, but the border was still due to open as planned. Then, on March 2, 2005, a lobby group of American ranchers convinced a judge to grant an injunction against the reopening. The border remained closed.

Where BSE leaves ranchers
When the border closed to live cattle, Alberta ranchers lost access to the American meat packing plants that had helped ensure packers in Alberta remained competitive. IBP in Lakeside and Cargill in High River are both American-owned companies that gained a near monopoly over the last decade

as they pushed smaller slaughter-houses out of business. Before the border closed, if packers up here were offering 70 cents and cattle across the line were 80 cents, Alberta ranchers loaded their cattle into trucks and sent them south. Since the border closed, Canada has seen a glut of cattle, insufficient slaughter capacity, and record-low prices. To make matters worse for ranchers, packing plants can keep their own herds and when ranchers try to hold out for better prices, packers just slaughter their own cattle and wait ranchers out.

As the BSE crisis deepened, consumers began to ask why prices weren't dropping in the grocery stores. Packers said they were dealing with increased costs as a result of testing. Ranchers were suffering as both feedlots and meat packers controlled their costs by paying less for cattle.

Albertans were outraged when the Auditor General released a report showing that packers saw a 281 percent increase in their profits in the second half of 2003. Income for Alberta farmers dropped by 43 percent that year.

Grant Hirsche raises Herefords near High River and is one of many ranchers who have come together to help cattle producers survive. "This country was built on the family farm," Hirsche says, "and we are in jeopardy of losing it." The effect of BSE has been devastating for the industry. "There's probably deeper and more long-term effects than anyone realizes," Hirsche says, warning that the impact on ranchers has put the producer side of the industry in danger of losing its viability.

4

"It's hard for government and industry to change," Hirsche says, explaining that the near-monopoly enjoyed by the big packers in Alberta increased the impact of BSE on producers. "Before BSE we were slowly becoming more dependent on these packers. The big packers moved in, and they put the little guys out of business – BSE just sped that up."

Two years after the border closed, the big Alberta packers kill 85 percent of Canadian cattle. The federal government has announced another $1 billion bailout but ranchers are asking for concrete steps instead of Band-Aids. "We need more competition," says Hirsche. As well as new packing plants, ranchers would like to see the government introduce legislation prohibiting packers from owning cattle as well as

instituting a minimum floor price for live cattle, a recommendation that was made in the Auditor General's 2004 report.

New meat packing plants are in the works. The Northwest Cattlemen's Alliance is proposing one for the heart of feedlot alley beside Lethbridge. Groups like the Canada Beef Export Federation are working to diversify the markets for Canadian beef and reduce our reliance on the United States.

Grant Hirsche and other Canadian producers have formed the Beef Initiative Group (BIF). Looking to the future, they are concerned about the ability of the big packers to put new plants out of business. The BIF is proposing a packing plant using innovative financing based on a model used in New Zealand where the producer end

of the industry is doing well. The BIF plant would respond to the demands of foreign consumers for mandatory BSE testing of all cattle slaughtered at the plant. The U.S. doesn't test all animals for BSE, so there is the potential to get a leg up over the U.S. in foreign markets through testing.

With the border still closed to live cattle, the need to build sufficient packing infrastructure in Canada is pressing, as is the need to diversify our export markets. In the meantime, Grant Hirsche has partnered with another local rancher to open their own butcher shop in Okotoks. With a steady stream of customers, they have found a ray of light in what has been a dark time for Alberta's cattle industry.

BSE: What is it?

Bovine spongiform encephalopathy gets its name from the sponge-like appearance of the brain of effected animals. BSE is one of a group of brain diseases affecting various animals and is caused when rogue proteins, called prions, start to mutate. The mutated prions trigger a chain reaction which eventually kills the original cell and then moves on to other cells. Holes form in the infected brain, crippling the affected animal and finally killing it. The only known source is animal feed contaminated from another diseased animal. The original source is believed to be feed containing tainted meat from sheep with a related disease called scrapie. The risk of transmission to humans is extremely small but once acquired, the disease is fatal.

BSE FAST FACTS

Number of cattle in Alberta in 2003:	5,220,000
Number of cattle in Alberta today:	5,930,000
Lowest prices since May 2003:	18 cents per pound for cull cattle, 63.6 cents per pound for fed and feeder cattle
2004 beef exports are up 25 percent from 2003, but still 18 percent below 2002 exports.	
2002 Alberta beef sales to Japan:	18,226 tonnes
2003 Alberta beef sales to Japan:	7,727 tonnes
Reduction in Canadian farm cash receipts between May 2003 and November 2004 due to border closure	$5 billion

1   Burger bus, Fort Kent.

2   Diane Llewelyn-Jones and
    12-year-old son Weston sell
    corn. It is Weston's first day
    on the job, Taber.

3   The Harty family, third generation
    grain farmers, unload their
    harvest, Aden.

4   (opposite page / top)
    Unloading grain at an Inland
    Terminal, Oyen.

5   (opposite page / bottom) The Inland
    Grain Terminal does what wooden
    grain elevators used to do. Here
    grain is weighed, graded and
    purchased, Falher.

→ (previous page) There are
80,000 bison in Alberta, more
than in any other province. The
herds are part of a rapidly
growing bison industry.

→ Alberta is a Canadian crop
leader, producing 46 percent
of Canada's barley, 34 percent
of her canola, 30 percent of the
country's wheat, 23 percent of
honey, and 100 percent of the
nation's sugar beets.

1   Farm implement shop, Thorsby.

2   Canola silos, Lloydminster. Oil seed processing company Archer Daniels Midland is one of the world's largest producers of soybeans, corn, wheat and cocoa. They process 1 million tonnes per year.

3   Alfalfa pellet plant worker at the largest alfalfa plant in Canada, Falher. Alfalfa grown on 45,000 acres is processed into pellets for livestock feed. One percent is used domestically and 99 percent is exported to Japan and Thailand. Before the drought hit hard in 2002 and 2003, they produced 140 tonnes annually but for the last two years their production has been drastically reduced to 75 tonnes per annum.

4   (opposite page) Hal Jorgensen, right, operations supervisor with VisionQuest Wind Energy, stands in their Castle River Wind Farm along with landowners, three generations of the Pincher Creek Hutterite Colony; Mike Gross, manager, his daughter Rosa and his granddaughter Valerie. The 67 wind turbines co-exist with regular farming operations and occupy less than two percent of the 2,400 acres, leaving farming routines virtually unaffected. Twelve of the 67 turbines provide enough power to run the entire C-Train transit system in Calgary. Vision Quest currently owns and operates 220 turbines with a total capacity of 190 megawatts, enough to power over 100,000 homes for a year.

→ Over 40 percent of farmers in Alberta use computers to manage their farms.

→ The Canadian alfalfa processing industry, also known as the dehydration industry, has matured over the past four decades to become the world's largest exporter of alfalfa pellets and the second largest exporter of alfalfa cubes behind the United States.

Alfalfa and other forage crops like hay and a variety of grasses are very important in soil conservation - they are used in crop rotation to improve soil structure, to add nitrogen to the soil and to hinder erosion.

→ In Canada, 40 percent of oil, 33 percent of margarine, 50 percent of shortening, and 75 percent of salad oil comes from canola.

Canola is also used in lip balms, sunscreens, insect repellents, newspaper ink and coffee whiteners.

Canola meal is fed to livestock and used in lawn fertilizers. Alberta produces 34 percent of Canada's canola.

→ Wind energy is among the fastest growing renewable energy technologies in the world and is the fastest growing renewable energy source in Canada.

As of December 2004, Canada's installed wind energy capacity was 444 megawatts.

Used to displace coal-generated electricity, this energy generation can displace the emission of roughly 850,000 tonnes of carbon dioxide into the atmosphere annually.

→ There are 53,000 farms covering 52 million acres.

1   (previous page) Sawmill in High Prairie. This stockpile of logs is from the 2003 harvest which happens in the winter months to help reduce the ecological impact.

2   Tree planters near Whitecourt.

3   Tree planters, High Prairie. Every summer young people come from all over Canada and around the world to plant trees.

4   Loading logs for processing at a sawmill near Fort Assiniboine.

5   Logging truck sign.

6   Logging trucker, Fox Creek.

→ Alberta covers over 66 million hectares of land; 59 percent or 38 million hectares is forested, making for about 2.2 billion cubic metres of growing stock.

→ The forest industry employs more than 25,000 people directly and supports employment for an additional 27,700 people.

→ Forestry is a primary industry in as many as 50 Alberta communities. Of those, 12 communities are deemed forestry dependent.

→ Each year 75 million seedlings are planted in Alberta.

→ One tonne of wood, sometimes referred to as a cord which is a stack measuring 4 ft x 4 ft x 8 ft, can produce:

   7,500,000 toothpicks
   942 books
   4,384,000 postage stamps
   12 dining room tables
   2,700 copies of the daily newspaper

One tonne of dry wood pulp can produce:

   0.9 tonnes of bathroom tissue
   1.05 tonnes of paperboard which can produce 1,400 lbs (636 kg) of magazine paper
   1 tonne of newsprint

→ Alberta owns approximately 87 percent of the province's forests and allows about 23.3 million cubic metres to be harvested annually. Another 9 percent of Alberta's forests are controlled by the federal government in the form of parks and other protected areas.

1   Loading a roll of newsprint, Red Deer.

2   (opposite page) Newspaper pressman, Red Deer.

3   (next spread) Pipeline crew, Hayter.

2

3

4

1　(opposite page) Oil patch
roughnecks near Manyberries.
A drilling rig usually has two
floorhands who are also called
roughnecks. They do much of
the heavy work at a well site.

2　Moving a service rig, Oyen.
A service rig is installed after the
drilling rig packs up and moves out.
The service rig crew runs tubing
down inside the casing, and
prepare the well for perforating.
This rig may also return to correct
any production problems the
well may have.

3　Pipeline crew, Buffalo.

4　Head office in Calgary.

→ Alberta is the ninth largest oil
producer in the world and the third
largest producer of natural gas.

→ Crude oil is a mixture of hundreds
of different hydrocarbon compounds
trapped in underground rock.
These hydrocarbons were created

millions of years ago when ancient
marine life or vegetation died and
settled on the bottoms of streams,
lakes, seas and oceans, forming
a thick layer of organic material.
Sediment later covered this layer,
applying heat and pressure that
"cooked" the organic material

and changed it into the petroleum
we extract from the ground today.
Conventional crude oil is produced
by drilling wells.

The deepest well ever drilled was
over 9.45 kms. In central Alberta,
wells average 1.5 to 1.7 kms.

→ There are 332,464 kms of
pipeline in Alberta.

→ Number of chemical compounds
released from the gas flares at oil
wells: 250.

→ Alberta produces five trillion
cubic feet of natural gas each year.

→ One in six Albertans are
employed directly or indirectly in
the energy sector, which translates
into more than 300,000 jobs.

→ The first gas pipeline in Alberta
began moving natural gas from
Bow Island to Calgary in 1912.

→ Natural gas travels through
pressurized pipelines at speeds of
40 kms per hour. It takes gas from
Alberta three days to reach
Ontario.

1   Gas plant near Crossfield.

2   Seismic worker, Edson.

3   Gas plant operators, Tees.

4   Terri Lynn Deveau, general manager of Quality Tubing Canada Ltd., serving the oil and gas industry worldwide from Red Deer.

5   Global Petroleum Show in Calgary.

6   Global Petroleum Show in Calgary.

7   (opposite page) Service rig workers near Bonneyville.

→ Natural gas is the largest single source of resource development revenue for Albertans, accounting for more than $21.8 billion in royalties paid to the government of Alberta from fiscal 2000-2001 to fiscal 2003-2004. This total represents about 70 percent of all provincial revenue from non-renewable resources over that period.

→ In 2003, there were 2,360 successful oil wells drilled in Alberta.

→ Alberta's crude oil and natural gas trade surplus contributed 57 percent of Canada's merchandise trade balance in 2003. Alberta produces more than 20 percent of North America's crude oil and natural gas but accounts for only 10 percent of its consumption.

→ Alberta exports more than 1 million barrels of oil to the United States every day.

→ Of the 68 large companies with headquarters in Calgary, all but five are in the energy sector.

→ Alberta's three oil sand deposits found at Athabasca, Cold Lake, and Peace River contain as much as 2.5 trillion barrels of bitumen – five times more than the conventional oil reserves in Saudi Arabia. The Athabasca deposit is twice the size of Lake Ontario.

Non-conventional crude oil is produced by upgrading a molasses-like substance called bitumen. The process involves mining, extracting and upgrading the bitumen contained in oil sands deposits.

→ It takes two tonnes of oil sand to produce a barrel of oil. Alberta's vast oil sands deposits contain 175 billion barrels of reserves. From 2000 to 2004, oil sands development grew dramatically with investment totaling over $28 billion. Oil sands production is currently about one million barrels per day and forecast to increase to 2.6 million barrels per day by 2015.

1   Unloading specially designed fuel
    truck for muskeg, High Level.

2   Mining the oil sands,
    Fort McMurray.

3   Loading fuel truck at the UFA
    in Beiseker.

4   Fuel truck driver, High Prairie.

5   Laying pipe, Fort McMurray.

6   Truck maintenance man
    for Syncrude, Fort McMurray.

7   (opposite page) Oil sands truck
    driver, Fort McMurray

→ Alberta's transportation infrastructure plays a critical role in the province's economy. The province's strength as a major exporter of primary commodities and manufactured products to the global marketplace is supported by a highly efficient and competitive transportation and logistics system.

Alberta has emerged as the western North American warehouse and distribution hub for Canada and the Pacific Northwest region of the United States. Alberta is the only western province that offers overnight, or less than 24-hour delivery service to all of western Canada and the U.S. Pacific Northwest. With direct connections to two of North America's largest highway trade corridors, quick and efficient access to the southern U.S. and Mexican markets is available.

→ The Alberta government maintains about 30,000 kms of provincial highways. Municipalities maintain approximately 137,298 kms of roads.

→ In 2003, Alberta workers reporting the highest number of back injuries were:
  · truck drivers
  · labourers
  · nurses
  · janitors and cleaners
  · freight handlers
  · carpenters
  · material handling labourers
  · welders and flame cutters

1 Heavy machinery mechanic, Hayter.

2 Welder, Linden.

3 Dustin fills up a jerry-can for a customer's boat at his summer job, Athabasca.

4 Metal worker, Linden.

5 Proud to be a steel worker, Ma-Me-O Beach.

6 Builders of flat deck trailers in Two Hills.

7 Gas-bar clerks, Lloydminster.

8 Vern's Garage, Edgerton.

9 Boyd Stevens of Stevens Hardware & Garage, Orion. Boyd has lived in Orion all of his life: " I missed the train - and then they took out the line."

10 Tire recyclers, Hythe.

→ Between 1993 and 2003, Alberta's manufacturing shipments increased by 123 percent to $45.8 billion.

Alberta's manufacturing sector is closely tied to the resource sector. About two-thirds of manufacturing output consists of value-added resource products.

→ Gasoline prices on March 22, 2005, in Canadian dollars

	Edmonton	Cdn average
Today	83.260	88.856
Yesterday	83.365	88.781
One Week Ago	83.322	87.319
One Month Ago	78.269	82.802
One Year Ago	73.968	77.110

→ Sales of fuel for road motor vehicles

In Alberta, in 2003	# litres
Net sales of gasoline	4,689,900,000
Gross sales of gasoline	4,984,600,000
Net sales of diesel oil	2,496,100,000

In Canada :	# litres
Net sales of gasoline	38,314,947,000
Gross sales of gasoline	39,691,024,000
Net sales of diesel oil	14,609,186,000

→ In 2005, 100,000 recycled tires were used to pave about 30 kms of road with asphalt rubber. The paving is part of a pilot project that has been underway since 2002 to determine if asphalt rubber is viable for Alberta.

Alberta is a leader in the field of asphalt rubber and is the only province in Canada to actively test asphalt rubber on its roads and highways. Asphalt rubber is a mixture of traditional asphalt cement, recycled tire crumb

and aggregate. It has been used in various ways by several countries over the last 15 years.

Since 1993, 30 million scrap tires have been recycled through Alberta's tire recycling program.

Since 2002, over 50 kms (including 2005 projects) of road have been paved with asphalt rubber pavement.

Results of the Alberta asphalt rubber test sections have shown a significant reduction in road noise. However, results are mixed in the area of cracking and surface condition. One of the biggest

challenges to asphalt rubber is Alberta's harsh winters and its large number of freeze-thaw days during spring which cause considerable stress to the pavement.

1 Big Tires at the Red Deer Air Show.

2 Flying over Edmonton.

3 Helicopter in the Drumheller Valley.

4 Hot air ballooning over Calgary.

5 RV club members, Torrington.

6 Steam Train approaching Big Valley.

7 Brian Haynes is in Wayne for the 20th annual Harley Davidson Appreciation Days. He's been going for twenty years.

8 Trick-jumping in Strathmore.

9 Demolition derby in Glendon.

→ Edmonton International Airport is Canada's most northerly 24-hour international airport and is situated at an elevation of 723 meters or 2372 feet above sea level. Edmonton International Airport handled 4,081,565 passengers in 2004 and is the fifth busiest airport in Canada in terms of passengers. It is the second largest airport in Canada by land mass as it comprises an area of just under 7,000 acres. The current runways are large enough to accommodate an immediate 200 percent growth in air traffic movements.

→ The Calgary International Airport is the fourth busiest Canadian airport with 1.5 million liters of fuel pumped daily and saw a total of 9,174,039 passengers in 2004.

→ In 2003, three people were killed and 35 people were injured in crashes in which trains were involved.

7

8

9

1

2

3

4

5

1   Slave Lake seadoo.

2   Edmonton Queen Riverboat Cruise.

3   Mudbog in Marwayne.

4   Going shopping in Caroline.

5   Albertans love their toys,
    Wandering River.

6   Boat leaving for five hour trip
    to Fort Chipewyan, Fort MacKay.

7   Long weekend traffic, Hwy 2.

8   Rafting down the Elbow River.

9   Mountain biking in the benchlands
    just outside of Canmore.

10 Canoeing in Waterton Park.

6

7

8

9

10

1   Motocross, Red Deer.

2   Highway 2.

3   Lac La Biche ice race.

4   Car repairs in Red Deer.

5   Race Trac Gas bikers, Chipman.

6   AC/DC car, Cold Lake.

7   Stunting; don't try this at home kids, Calgary.

8   Stock car races in Red Deer.

9   Dodge, Chevy, Ford gathering in Edgerton.

10 Antique mini-car dealer in Red Deer.

11 (next spread) Metal recyclers, Calgary.

→ In 2003, there were 13 people killed in collisions involving motorcycles. Motorcycle drivers under the age of 25 were most likely to be involved in casualty collisions. Compared to drivers in total casualty collisions, motorcycle drivers were more likely to run off the road or pass improperly.

→ In 2003, there were 76 people killed and 782 injured in collisions involving truck tractors. Compared to drivers of other vehicles, truck tractor drivers were more likely to run off the road, but less likely to have consumed alcohol.

→ Rank of Alberta among provinces for truck sales per capita: 1

→ The replacement value of the provincial highway network is estimated to be $19.6 billion.

→ The CANAMEX Trade Corridor links Canada, the United States, and Mexico with a 6,000-kilometre stretch of highway from Alaska to Mexico City. In Alberta, the 1,175-kilometre North-South Trade Corridor runs from Coutts to the Alaska Highway. Since the North American Free Trade Agreement (NAFTA) was signed in 1993, Alberta's trade with the United States has increased by 400 percent and trade with Mexico has jumped by 900 percent.

6

7

8

9

10

→ (previous spread) Sources of waste metals consist primarily of residential and commercially generated items such as steel and aluminum cans, white goods (fridges, stoves), small appliances and other miscellaneous items (metal furnishings, fasteners and fittings). Most sources of scrap metals are not considered part of the municipal solid waste stream as they have traditionally been recovered for recycling due to their high value and are unlikely to end up in landfill. Steel made from recycled scrap uses only one-quarter of the energy it takes to make steel from its primary resource, iron ore. Aluminum can be recycled at savings of up to 95 percent of the energy used to manufacture it from aluminum ore. Close to 75 percent of ferrous scrap (steel) and 45 percent of non-ferrous scrap (aluminum, brass, copper) are recovered for recycling.

→ In Alberta there are 2,364,402 licensed drivers, driving 2,379,910 registered motor vehicles. This excludes trailers, off-highway vehicles, dealer or antique plated vehicles.

→ There are 3,767 bridges on Alberta highways and 8,675 bridges on municipal roads.

→ "When Solomon said there was a time and a place for everything, he had not encountered the problem of parking his automobile." - Bob Edwards.

→ Pedestrians between the ages of 15 and 19 were found to be most likely to be involved in a crash. Pedestrian casualty collisions were most likely to occur during the evening rush hour.

→ About 80 percent of Alberta's population of 3,212,813 reside in urban centres. In 1906 the population was 185,412, with only 31 percent of Albertans living in urban centres. (An urban dweller is defined as living within a municipality of 1000 or more residents.)

→ Population density in Alberta (people per square kilometer): 4.6; in Ontario: 12.6; in Hong Kong: 6,668

In Alberta During 2003...
- 385 people were killed as a result of traffic collisions
- 26,426 people were injured in traffic collisions
- A total of 113,357 collisions occurred

Every day in 2003 approximately...
- 1 person was killed
- 72 people were injured
- 311 traffic collisions were reported

→ Calgary is Canada's second largest head office city, while Edmonton is the location of most of Alberta's provincial and federal government offices. Office occupancy costs for both cities have consistently been among the lowest, compared to other major metropolitan areas in Canada.

→ **Geographic area of Edmonton:** 9,419 square kilometers; **of Calgary:** 5,083 square kilometers; **of New York City:** 785 square kilometers

→ As the population in Alberta continues to rise, rural populations are declining – a phenomenon across the country. The true effects of rural depopulation are yet to be fully understood – it is alarming, to say the least.

→ The retail trade industry employed about 203,000 Albertans in 2004. The industry is expected to grow by a yearly average of 2 percent, employing about 223,200 people in 2009.

The 2004 unemployment rate in the retail trade was 3.9 percent (the average for all industries was 4.6 percent). Alberta experienced recent growth in retail trade fuelled by low interest rates and employment growth. It is expected this growth will slow down slightly before picking up again. The threat of rising interest rates may curb consumer spending. Another

potential challenge is worker shortages especially in northern areas where retail is picking up as a spin-off of oil and gas activity. Higher wages in the construction, mining, and oil and gas industries lure labour away from the retail industry.

2

3

4

5

6

7

1   (opposite page) Construction worker working on the redevelopment of Sir Winston Churchill Square, Edmonton.

2   Steel workers, Calgary.

3   Building sidewalk, Manning.

4   Earth movers remove black-top in preparation of a new subdivision in Okotoks.

5   Concrete crew, Calgary.

6   Crane operator IBM building, Calgary.

7   Building sidewalk in Langdon.

→ Many Edmontonians criticized the $12.6 million redevelopment of Sir Winston Churchill Square as being too lavish and a waste of money.

→ Alberta's construction sector is made up of both general and specialty contracting firms and trades people. They are engaged in industrial, commercial, institutional and residential construction. They also handle infrastructure projects, renovation and repairs as well as providing maintenance services.

Alberta's construction sector includes both union and non-union trades people.

→ Over $96 billion in major capital projects are proposed, announced, under construction or recently completed as of November 2004.

→ Construction contracting is a large and diverse industry. General contractor employment is approximately 40 percent of the industry with specialty trades contractors comprising the balance. Spin-off benefits to other sectors from construction are high. Labour generally runs about a third of construction costs.

1   Sign about new school being
built, Calmar.

2   Sandblasting, Syncrude.

3   Workers waiting for bus that takes
them to their work site in the tar
sands, Fort McMurray.

4   Plant in Exshaw.

5   Wind turbine under construction,
Magrath.

6   (opposite page) Concrete workers,
Falher

→ Architecture, engineering
and construction (AEC) employs
nearly 150,000 people in over
6000 businesses. The large
percentage of architects,
engineers, technologists,
project managers and skilled
trades people in the AEC sector
enjoy relatively high pay and
quality employment. The annual
revenue of the AEC sector
approaches $13 billion.

→ "The Calgary-Edmonton
Corridor is Canada's western
tiger.... Given all of its assets, the
Corridor enjoys enormous
potential – not only to widen its
economic lead within Canada, but
to become the region that stands
out as the most prosperous and
best place to live in all of North
America."
- TD Bank Financial Group,
TD Economics Special Report April 22, 2003

1   Mennonite construction crew,
    Brooks.

2   House framer, Fort McMurray.

3   Roofing west of Calgary.

4   Building luxury home just
    south of Calgary.

5   A family home under construction,
    Pinehurst.

6   Building a 27 storey high-rise
    condo development.

7   (opposite page) House framer,
    south of Calgary.

8   (next spread) Engineman,
    Whitecourt.

→ According to Statistics Canada, there were 36,270 housing starts in 2004 in Alberta - about 16 percent of Canada's total.

→ Data compiled by the financial arm of one of the country's big banks puts Alberta near the top of the list when it comes to housing affordability. Alberta's reign as one of the most affordable regions in which to own a house is expected to continue through 2004, says the Royal Bank of Canada's Financial Group.

The report is a bit deceiving, however. At first glance, its conclusions suggest house prices in Alberta and even Calgary are low compared to other parts of Canada, which isn't true by a long shot.

A detached bungalow – RBC's benchmark home for first-time buyers – costs $134,250 in Atlantic Canada. That same house in Calgary – minus the ocean view – will set a buyer back $228,099, almost $100,000 more. A buyer will fork over $303,901 for that bungalow in Toronto and in Vancouver it will cost $325,622.

The report charts and establishes its index using average household incomes, which fluctuate from city to city as much as house prices do. Calgary's advantage then, according to the report, is that the average income here – at $59,314 – is higher than all other Canadian cities with the exception of Toronto at $59,674. Vancouver's average is $51,676.

"It's definitely the other important part of the equation and in Alberta (where the average income is $54,089), and especially Calgary, it makes the big difference," the report says. In other words, owning a home here is more reasonable partially because Albertans make more money.

1   (opposite page) Flagman,
    La Corey.

2   Garbage men, Rainbow Lake.

3   Grader operator, Grouard

4   Linemen, near Bonnyville.

5   Land surveyors, High Prairie.

6   Snow plow operator, Lac La Biche.

→ Revenues for Alberta's information and communications technology industry totalled approximately $9 billion in 2003. Alberta Supernet, to be completed in 2005, is a government initiative to provide highspeed, broadband access to 429 Alberta communities.

→ Alberta's labour force consists of over 1.8 million well-educated workers. In 2003, 57.9 percent of the labour force who were 25 years of age and older reported holding a university degree, post-secondary diploma or certificate. In addition, Alberta has the highest work force participation rate at 73.4 percent, compared to the national average of 67.5 percent.

→ An estimated 80 percent of material currently disposed of at landfills is recoverable through composting (organics) and recycling (paper, cardboard, metal, plastic, glass).

About one-tenth of the average weekly shopping bill is spent on packaging alone. The challenge is to reverse the current waste hierarchy by moving away from waste disposal and toward pollution prevention, waste reduction, reuse and recycling.

Two or three bags of garbage per household doesn't sound like much, but it works out to nearly 500 kilograms of garbage per person in Alberta. When you add commercial and industrial waste, it works out to an average of one tonne for each man, woman and child in the province.

→ Alberta spends about $179 million a year on highway maintenance.

→ Year the first official hand-lettered roadsigns were installed in Alberta: 1923. Percentage increase in size of letters on roadsigns between 1923 and now: 40

1   Insurance agents, Valleyview.

2   Roofing crew, Andrew Post Office.

3   Youngstown Village office.

4   Loading fuel destined for Fort
    Chipewyan via Air Mikisew,
    Fort McMurray.

5   Post office assistant, Grouard.

6   Post Mistress, Buffalo.

7   Delivery lady sorting mail,
    Clairmont.

8   (opposite page) Post Mistress,
    Heinsburg.

→ The percentage of unionized
workers in Alberta is the lowest
among all provinces:
Canada: 32 percent;
Alberta: 22 percent

→ Number of **cities** in Alberta:
15; **towns:** 110; **villages:** 104;
summer villages: 52

→ Canada Post has just over 7,000
employees in Alberta.

There are about 650 postal
outlets in the province. (This
includes corporate offices as
well as franchise outlets in host
businesses). Nationally, Canada
Post delivers 37 million pieces
of mail per day.

→ Average annual full-time income
in Alberta: **men:** $51,116; **women:**
$33,185

Rank of Alberta among provinces
with the highest proportion of
women working: 1

Rank of Alberta among provinces
with the widest income gap
between men and women: 1

1   Fighting a residential fire in Calgary.

2   Rapid Attack Patrol Firefighters,
    Rainbow Lake.

3   Firefighter fun at the annual
    firefighter's tug-of-war, Longview.

4   Erlton fire, Calgary.

5   Firefighter, Calgary.

6   Water bomber ground crew,
    High Level airport.

7   Firefighter training centre,
    Vermilion.

8   Firefighter ground crew,
    Steen River Firefighter Camp.

9   Fire lookout person, Puskwaskau
    lookout tower, near Valleyview.

10 (next spread) Red Deer Westerner
    Days Parade.

→ Residential fires cause approximately $51 million worth of damage every year in Alberta. Out of all the fire deaths in the province, 65 percent were from residential fires, with careless cooking the number one cause of residential fires.

→ In 1959, one hundred emergency call boxes were installed in downtown Edmonton, making Edmonton the third city in Canada to allow citizens to call fire, ambulance or police from public phones.

→ In Alberta in 2003, the 2,000 employed firefighters and over 9,500 volunteer firefighters fought 5,614 fires - that's about 15 fires every day. These did not include grass fires or wildfires (also known as forest fires).

→ Firefighters make up about 4 percent of the total deaths caused by fires in Alberta.

→ Following 2004's severe wildfires in the northern part of the province, Albertans are reminded to take extra care while handling fire in and around Alberta's forested areas.

→ In 2004 the Government of Alberta spent approximately $198 million battling more than 1,600 wildfires across the province. Those fires burnt nearly 235,000 hectares of land, much of which was located in northern Alberta.

8

9

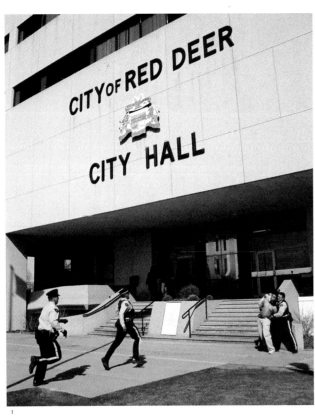

1   RCMP officers had their hands full on April 20, International Marijuana Day, Red Deer.

2   RCMP National memorial, Edmonton.

3   Opening ceremonies, Alberta 2005 Summer Games, High River.

4   RCMP officers in Peace River.

5   Fort Macleod musical ride.

6   RCMP raising money for the Red Deer Women's Shelter, Red Deer.

7   Keeping the peace at the Calgary Stampede.

8   Stables at Fort Macleod.

9   Canada Day musical ride, Banff

→ There are some 2,600 men and women serving the **RCMP in Alberta** today.

The **Calgary Police Service** is made up of more than 1,400 police officers and 550 civilian members.

The **Edmonton Police Service** employs over 1,196 sworn police officers and 326 civilian members.

Approximately 182 people make up the **Lethbridge Regional Police Service** with 130 of those sworn police officers.

The **Blood Reserve Police Service** is comprised of 32 sworn peace officers with 17 civilian support staff.

The **Camrose** and **Medicine Hat Police Service** statistics were unavailable at the time of printing.

7

8

9

1,2,3 National Memorial Service, Edmonton.

→ On March 3, 2005, four RCMP officers were shot and killed while investigating stolen property and a marijuana grow operation near Mayerthorpe, 130 kms north of Edmonton. Their killer, suspect James Roszko, also shot himself.

It was the single worst multiple killing of RCMP officers in modern Canadian history.

"You'd have to go back to 1885, to the Northwest Rebellion, to have a loss of this magnitude. It's devastating," said RCMP Assistant Commissioner Bill Sweeney.

The officers who lost their lives were Constable Peter Schiemann, 25; Constable Anthony Gordon, 28; Constable Lionide Johnston, 34; and Constable Brock Myrol, 29.

The community of Mayerthorpe reeled in shock as condolences poured in from across the country. Mayor Albert Schalm said RCMP officers in small towns aren't strangers to the people they serve. "They're your neighbours, they're your friends, you curl with them, you play hockey with them," said Schalm.

3

One week later, thousands of police officers from across the country and the United States joined mourners and dignitaries inside Edmonton's Butterdome to honor the fallen men in the largest memorial service in the Mounties' history.

Governor General Adrienne Clarkson painted a personal picture of the men who Canadians had come to know in such a tragic manner. "We now know," she said, "as they do in Whitecourt, that Tony Gordon was an outdoorsman, about to become a father for the second time. In Mayerthorpe, they likely knew, as we do now, that Leo Johnston was a newlywed, and had joined the RCMP on the same day as his twin brother; that Peter Schiemann was a keen curler with a big smile and strong faith. They hadn't had much time to learn about the rookie, Brock Myrol, with his black belt in karate and new fiancée."

Clarkson praised the Mounties' service and urged all to "remember those who have given everything." Family and friends of the four officers remembered the men in moving tributes and described their pride in belonging to the RCMP.

In Mayerthorpe, residents gathered around TV sets and radios to watch or listen to the memorial, which was broadcast nationally.

"There are going to be a lot of sad days ahead for a lot of us," said Leo Bablitz, who owns a hardware store in town.

1

2

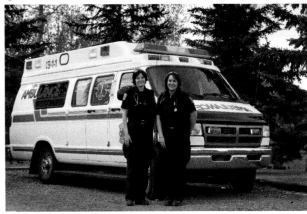

3

1   STARS air ambulance, Calgary.

2   20th Field Regiment, Red Deer.

3   EMS, Andrew Alberta division,
Ukrainian Cultural Heritage Village.

4   Canadian Armed Forces soldier
saluting, Wainwright.

5   Canadian Armed Forces loading
dummy missel in training exercise.

6   Canadian Armed Forces,
F18 Pilots, Cold Lake.

7   (opposite page) Canadian Armed
Forces, weapon loading crew,
Cold Lake.

4

5

6

→ The Alberta Shock Trauma Air Rescue Society (STARS) is dedicated to providing a safe, rapid, highly specialized emergency aero-medical transport system for critically ill and injured patients. It is a non-profit organization that, in 2002, flew 1,115 missions, carrying only critically ill or injured patients.

STARS prime concern is appropriate medical care delivered to the patient in the most timely way possible. In a 250-km radius around Calgary and Edmonton, ground ambulance or STARS helicopters are the fastest mode of transport.

→ In Alberta there are 9 regional health authorities, 1 health board, 29.7 million square feet of facility space with a $6.25 billion replacement cost.

→ The Canadian Armed Forces includes the army, navy and air force .

→ The Canadian federal budget for 2005 represents the most significant investment in the military in over 20 years.

→ The army's 19,500 regular and 15,500 reserve soldiers are actively serving Canadians in today's unstable and unpredictable world. Of these, 2,033 are women. Almost 4,000 soldiers a year deploy on missions to places like Bosnia, Kosovo, East Timor, Ethiopia and Afghanistan. Their task is to restore peace and represent Canada internationally. The army is also prepared to assist provincial and territorial authorities with natural disasters including earthquakes, floods, storms and forest fires.

→ Currently, more than 1,600 Canadian soldiers, sailors and air force personnel are deployed overseas on operational missions. On any given day, about 8,000 Canadian Forces members - one third of our deployable force - are preparing for, engaged in or returning from an overseas mission.

1 Cadets singing Oh Canada during the Royal Visit 2005, Edmonton.

2 Viewing the inside of a tank, Calgary.

3 Border Guard, Trevor Carruthers, has been at the Wildhorse border crossing for about a year. During the summer up to 40 cars may cross the border per day, in the winter about 10 cars cross; but, he says, "there are a lot of rattlesnakes."

4 Pilots signing autographs, Red Deer Air Show.

5 Conservation officer searching for fossil poachers in Dinosaur Provincial Park. Poaching is quite an issue in the park.

6 Rat Control, Lloydminster, "We haven't seen a rat in this country for two and a half years".

7 Ranger in Cypress Hills.

8 Conservation officer checking for fishing licenses, Sylvan Lake.

→ The Department of Defence's "immediate family" comprises more than 100,000 Canadians, including the members of the regular and reserve force, the Canadian Rangers and the civilian employees of the department.

The department also supports the Canadian Cadet Movement and the Junior Canadian Rangers.

These include:
62,000 members of the regular force
22,000 members of the reserve force
20,000 civilians
3,600 Canadian Rangers

The family also includes 2,100 Junior Canadian Rangers, 60,000 Cadets, 130,000 members of military families, thousands of workers in defence-related industries, and hundreds of thousands of veterans and pensioners. In all, approximately half a million Canadians belong to the extended defence family.

→ There are six International Ports of Entry via Alberta highways:

1. Aden, AB - U.S. Port: Whitlash, MT
2. Carway, AB - U.S. Port: Peigan, MT
3. Chief Mountain, AB - U.S. Port: Chief Mountain, MT
4. Coutts, AB - U.S. Port: Sweetgrass, MT
5. Del Bonita, AB - U.S. Port: Del Bonita, MT
6. Wildhorse, AB - U.S. Port: Wildhorse, MT

There are over 200 million crossings per year between the USA and Canada.

5

6

7

8

→ The five national parks in Alberta occupy a total of 63,045 square kms, the largest area in any province.

National Parks	Square Kms.
Banff	6,641
Elk Island	194
Jasper	10,878
Waterton Lakes	525
Wood Buffalo	44,807
TOTAL	**63,045**

There are also:	No.	Hectares
Provincial Parks	68	208,767.2
Provincial Recreation Areas	248	81,926.1
Ecological Reserves	16	29,444.4
Wilderness Areas	3	100,988.8
Natural Areas	150	143,523.5
Willmore Wilderness Park	1	459,671.0
Other	32	1,728,648.0
TOTAL	**518**	**2,752,969.0**

1   Hot air ballon pilot, over Calgary.

2   Railroad engineer, Stettler
    steam train between Stettler
    and Big Valley.

3   Doormen at the Palliser Hotel,
    Calgary.

4   Helicopter pilot, High Level.

5   Taxi cab driver,
    Calgary International Airport.

6   (opposite page) Eric Eaton,
    an interpreter at Heritage Park,
    Calgary

→ There are up to 5,000 taxi or limousine drivers in Alberta.

→ As rail lines disappear across the prairie and passenger trains are far and few between, thousands of eager passengers ride the Alberta Prairie Steam Train that runs between Stettler and Big Valley. Formed in 1990, Alberta Prairie ran under an operating agreement over rail lines owned by Central Western Railway Corporation, the very first short-line railway chartered in Canada by the federal government. In 1997, following a series of rail abandonment's by CWR, brought on by the rationalization of the grain handling system and the disappearance of the "Crow" benefit to agriculture, the 21.2 miles of track between Stettler and Big Valley that APST currently operates on was purchased by the East Central Alberta Heritage Society. That society was a creation of local municipalities eager to maintain some rail in the area on which Alberta Prairie could continue to offer excursion service.

→ Tourism supports just over 120,000 jobs in Alberta, about half directly in the industry and half indirectly.

1   Housekeepers, Fox Creek.

2   Alan Poirier and Dan Parker are interpreters at the Medicine Hat Clay Industries National Historic District.

3   Hotel kitchen staff, Calgary.

4   Server at the Alberta Sports Hall of Fame 2004 Induction Dinner.

5   Chefs enjoy a quiet moment before the storm on Stampede Parade morning behind 8th Avenue, Calgary.

6   (opposite page) Don Zimmer with son Earl own and operate the Sleepy Hollow Campground in Pincher Creek.

7   (next spread / left) Currency exchange and food store, Coutts.

8   (next spread / right) Grocery store owner, Grouard.

→ The accommodation and food services industry employed about 121,600 people in Alberta in 2003.

→ There are over 1,000 campgrounds in Alberta.

1   (opposite page) Stevens hardware and Garage, Orion.

2   Jeny Davis owns and operates the local store in Picture Butte.

3   Maria Kranjcevic, certified beautician. In 2004, Maria celebrated 27 years in Calgary's little Italy neighbourhood, "I always wanted to be a hair dress and look at me now!" I plan to stay here as long as I can, but they're tearing a lot of buildings down around here, so I don't know how long I'll be here, hopefully for a while."

4   Warburg food store owners.

5   Gundy's Beaver Mines Store, Beaver Mines.

6   Convenient store clerk, Calgary.

7   Salvation Army workers, Brooks.

8   Captain Morgan, Calgary.

→ There are up to 5,000 storekeepers in Alberta.

→ Alberta is the only province that does not have a provincial retail sales tax.

→ The first store opened in Alberta in 1778. It was a trading post, built by Pete Pond of Montreal and was situated about 30 miles from Lake Athabasca on the Athabasca River.

→ The first food bank in Canada opened its doors on January 16, 1981 in Edmonton.

→ As Calgary's population grows, the number of homeless has also increased.

The city conducted an in-depth survey, their research showed a substantial increase in homelessness, for a total of 2,597 persons. Of those, 77 percent were male, 23 percent female and there were more than 100 families.

Alderman Bob Hawkesworth said a lack of affordable housing is one problem and he blames government funding cuts. "The fact that the province cancelled housing programs in the early nineties in my view has been a contributing factor to the growth of homelessness."

Agencies like the Mustard Seed Street Ministry are calling on the Klein government to step up funding for low cost housing, increase the assured income program and raise Alberta's minimum wage.

1

2

3

4

5

6

7

1   Woody's Book Shack owner and operator, Sheryl Middleton, Medicine Hat.

2   Seamstresses, Calgary.

3   Marv's Classic Soda Shop is Canada's only soda fountain. The cash register is from 1905, Black Diamond.

4   Sausage for sale at a Calgary Stampeder football game, Calgary.

5   Summer Dayze Kettle Korn Company, here at the Millarville Market.

6   Fruit stand, Edmonton.

7   Tim Horton's cashiers, Cold Lake.

8   Corianne Jenner, owner of Swirl, aesthetics, massage and natural products, Calgary.

9   Western Coffee Shop, Calgary.

10 Medicine man, Calgary.

→ Amount Albertans spend on wine, beer and liquor annually: $1,000,000,000 – the highest among provinces per capita.

1   Liquor store owner, Sexsmith.

2   Evelyn Webster is a familiar face at the Manyberries Hotel.

3   Bar in Okotoks.

4   Turning the rye barrels at the Alberta Distillers Limited, Calgary.

5   (opposite page) Mike Tymchuk, Master Brewer and owner of the WildRose Brewing Company, Calgary.

1   Windsor Salt warehouse
    near Lindbergh.

2   Llama show, Red Deer.

3   Certified blacksmith gives
    demonstrations at Heritage
    Park, Calgary

4   Flute builders, Canmore.

5   Folding newspapers, Red Deer.

6   (opposite page) Craftspeople
    selling their wares at the
    Millarville Market.

WHAT IS HYPERTUFA?

It is a man-made product that looks like rock, yet is made of cement, peat moss, and perlite. It is light weight and very porous and it is ideal for annuals.

1   Handcrafted birdfeeders, Calgary.

2   Wedding photographer, Edmonton.

3   Artist and her summer student
    paint murals in Bow Island.

4   Roadside carpet and flag dealer,
    Red Deer.

5   (opposite page) Handcrafted
    signs, Millarville Market.

Please
NO NUDE
SWIMMING
SUNBATHING
VOLLEYBALL
ON BEACH

HANDPAINTED DECOR SIGNS
ANTIQUE REPRODUCTIONS
CUSTOM DESIGNS ★ ADVERTISING
HOME ★ CAFE ★ BUSINESS DECOR
Nanton Alberta 646-3214

HIPPIES
Please
**USE BACK
DOOR**

**NO
SKINNY
DIPPING**

HERB GARDEN

SUNSET DR
THEATRE
EDMONTON TRAIL
FRIDAY AND SAT.

Please
**DO NOT
FEED
BEARS**
BANFF BYLAW 27 Aug 1993

BREAKFAST
Early Bird Specials

Experienced
Waitress
WANTED

**NUDE
BEACH**

**CAUTION
WILD
BUFFALO**

**"NO
NUDES**

SPORTSMEN:
**FLY FISHING ONLY
IN THIS STREAM**
Bait and Lures
Not Permitted

FULL TIM
Dishwa
WANTE
APPLY WITHIN

BEWAR
BULL IN
PASTURE

- NOTICE -
WILD HORSES
IN
PASTURE
Please Keep Gate Closed!

ANGLE

MERCANTILE

ABCDEFGHIJKLMNOPQRSTUVWXYZ
ZYXWVUTSRQPONMLKJIHGFEDCBA

**NO
HUNTING**

**NO
SKINNY
DIPPING**

Experienced
Waitress
WANTED

**CANOE
RENTALS**
• DAILY • HOURLY • WEEKLY

**FARM
EGGS**

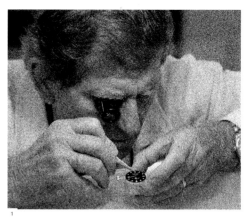

1 Rolex repairman, Edmonton.

2 Saw filer, High Prairie.

3 Handcrafted shields and swords, Bragg Creek.

4 Green Fools, a physical theatre troop, specialists in puppetry, stilt walking and performance art, Calgary.

5 (opposite page) Grave digger, Morinville.

6 (next spread / left) Shoe repairman, Red Deer.

7 (next spread / right) Saddle maker, Warner

1   Rodeo clown, Cold Lake.

2   Media, Calgary Stampede infield.

3   Flagman at the chuckwagon races,
    Calgary Stampede.

4   Jockey at the 99th annual
    Millarville Races.

5   Outrider at the Strathmore Rodeo.

6   Photographers capturing the
    Royal Visit 2005 in Edmonton.

7   Cameraman at the 2004 annual
    Labour Day football game between
    the Edmonton Eskimos and the
    Calgary Stampeders. The Eskies
    won this game.

→ Rodeos are deeply rooted in
the social fabric all across Alberta
– an array of jobs are created by
a rodeo – and just about every
community has one.

1   2004 Labour Day CFL game.

2   2004 Labour Day CFL game.

3   Officials at the 2004 Alberta
    Summer Games, Okotoks.

4   (following page) 2004 Labour
    Day CFL game.

→ Today, there are over 863 registered certified veterinarians practicing in over 350 veterinary clinics throughout Alberta.

→ As of December 31, 2003 there were 5,869 physicians currently registered in Alberta with the College of Physicians and Surgeons of Alberta

* 2,697 received undergraduate training in Alberta.
* 1,529 received undergraduate training in other parts of Canada.

* 1,643 received undergraduate training outside of Canada.

1   Doctor treating photographer for dog bite, Slave Lake.

2   Veterinarian Karen and assistant Sydney tend to animals like Rozzi at the Canmore Veterinary Hospital.

3   Premier Ralph Klein, Edmonton.

4   Premier Ralph Klein signing autographs at the annual Premier's Pancake Breakfast, Edmonton.

5   Mayor of Vulcan; his town is home to the annual Star Trek Convention.

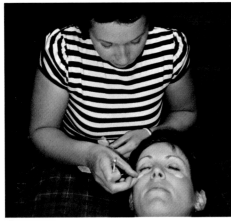

1 Daycare worker walking kids, Edmonton.

2 Auctioneer at the 2004 Alberta Sports Hall of Fame Inductee Dinner, Red Deer.

3 DJ on New Years Eve, Calgary.

4 Aesthetician giving a facial, Calgary.

5 Virginia Ann in her "Artists Cabin", Harvey Heights near Canmore.

6 (opposite page) Garbage collectors at the Calgary Stampede

1   Young man working at Red Deer's
    Westerner Days.

2   Clown at the Pincher Creek Kite
    Festival near Old Man Dam.

3   Harvey at Strathmore Rodeo.

4   Calgary Stampede.

5   The Howdys, Calgary Stampede.

6   Event worker at Capri Centre,
    Red Deer.

7   Bronco Buddy at Longview's
    annual New York Daze.

8   Carni worker, Klondike Days,
    Edmonton.

THE HOWDYS

2

1   Interpreter at the Etzikom
Windmill Museum.

2   Volunteer at the Millarville
chuckwagon races.

1   Volunteers at the Bow Island
    Tourist Information Centre.

2   Public outreach Unicef Workers,
    Edmonton.

3   Volunteer and Director of the
    Strathmore Rodeo.

4   Moderator and race official,
    both volunteers at the 99th annual
    Millarville Races.

5   Firefighters enjoy a tug of war,
    Longview

6   (opposite page) Missionaries from
    the USA, living in Alberta and
    spreading their word. Medicine Hat.

→ Canadians have a rich history of volunteering and community involvement. From soup kitchens to volunteer fire departments, helpful neighbours to dedicated drivers, volunteers are part of Canada's way of life. More than

6.5 million Canadians use their knowledge, skills, abilities, talents and interests to contribute to their communities. Teaching a young person life skills, coaching gymnastics, coordinating a fundraising event, cleaning up

a park, helping out in an emergency—there are endless ways that Canadians get involved.

→ Four out of 10 Albertans volunteered either formally with an organization for activities

such as canvassing, organizing events, and delivering food to the needy; or informally on their own in activities such as babysitting, doing yard work, and driving someone to an appointment.

→ Albertans are more likely than other Canadians to volunteer (40 percent of Albertans versus 31.4 percent of Canadians). Albertans contribute 127 million hours—the equivalent of more than 67,000 full time year-round jobs.

The average Albertan contributes 139 hours each year to causes they believe in, including organizing activities or events, fundraising, working on committees, coaching, and providing care and support to others.

Alberta Faces

We gather, we meet, we play, we laugh, we cry, we stop and think and rejoice in the moments when we are not at work – whatever we do – that thing called life.

1   Three boys goof around at the 4-H
    rodeo in Czar.

1   (opposite page) An emotive crowd
    at the annual Labour Day football
    match between the Edmonton
    Eskies and the Calgary Stamps,
    Calgary.

2   White hats at the Stampede
    Parade, Calgary.

3   3-D movie goers at The Uptown
    Screen, Calgary.

4   Ukrainian Catholic Church Of The
    Assumption Of The Blessed Virgin
    Mary at the 100 Year Jubilee of

the Basilian Fathers and Sisters
Servants of Mary Immaculate Of
Pastoral and Missionary Service in
Canada. Star/Peno. This is the first
Catholic Ukrainian Parish in Canada.

5   Crowds gather at the Red Deer
    Air Show.

6   National Aboriginal Day,
    Head-Smashed-In Buffalo Jump
    Interpretive Centre - a UNESCO
    World Heritage Site.

1   Crowd gathered at Edmonton's
    100 year celebrations in 2004.

2   Stampede Grounds, Calgary.

3   Canmore Folk Festival.

4   Crowd gathered to watch events at
    the 2004 Arctic Winter Games in
    Fort McMurray.

5   (opposite page / top)
    Strathmore Rodeo.

6   (opposite page / bottom)
    Riders arrive at the 20th annual
    Harley Davidson Appreciation
    Days, Wayne.

1 Proud Canadian kids at the Grand Prairie Canada Day celebrations.

2 Filipino Association Canada Day Float, Grand Prairie.

3 Picnic at the Manyberries rodeo grounds.

4 13th annual Galaxyfest - Year of the Klingon - part of the annual Spockdays in Vulcan. Klingons, Borgs, Romulans and other species join the Vulcans in celebrating Spockdays.

5 Indoor Rodeo in Hanna.

6 60th anniversary of D-Day, Turner Valley.

7 Snow Drag Racers at the Renyolds Museum, Wetaskwin.

8 90th anniversary of Canada's worst-ever mine disaster in Hillcrest. On June 19, 1914, 189 men lost their lives.

9 (next spread) Every year thousands of passengers ride the Alberta Prairie steam train on the 34-kilometer excursion that runs from Stettler to Big Valley, and back again.

5

6

7

8

1   (opposite page) On the midway
      at the Calgary Stampede.

2   Fireworks at Lac La Biche days.

3   Fear Factor event in Vulcan.

4   Hypnotist Robert Messmer
      mesmerizes these participants
      at Westerner Days, Red Deer.
      Quite remarkable.

5   Fair ride at Klondike Days.

6   He's not alone, at least, selling
      his wares, Millarville.

7   Fair ride at the Stampede, Calgary.

1　20th annual Harley Davidson Appreciation Days in Wayne.

2　Fort Normandeau Days on the banks of the Red Deer River.

3　Actors entertain thousands of visitors at Heritage Park, Calgary.

4　Fort Edmonton Trolly Car Operator.

5　Harvest Days, Reynolds Museum, Wetaskwin.

6　Trekkies pose with the characters from Star Trek, Vulcan Starship.

7　The burn-out pit, Wayne.

8　Klondike Days Tub Race in downtown Edmonton.

9　Every event has these...

10　Adults playing arcade games, Red Deer.

11　(next spread / right) Her Majesty Queen Elizabeth II, Queen of Canada, does a walk-about in the Legislature gardens in Edmonton

12　(next spread / left) Holding Canadian flag at Peigen Powwow.

7

8

9

10

1 Provincial flag at the Cold Lake
   Rodeo, Cold Lake.

2 Waving flags, Fort McMurray.

3 Gas plant operators, Tees.

4 Norweigen flag, near Beaverlodge.

5 Rocky Mountain House RCMP
   Detachment 2004 Regimental Ball.

6 D-Day, Turner Valley.

7 Village of Rosemary office,
   Rosemary.

8 Flag bearers at Alberta Summer
   Games opening ceremonies,
   High River.

9 Window in Red Deer.

10 (next spread) Chief in convertible
   in the 90th Annual Calgary
   Stampede, 2002.

1   (next spread) 2nd Annual Running of the Bulls, Strathmore Rodeo.

1   Couple on bulls, Rockyford.

2   Chuckwagon Races, Strathmore.

3   Muttan-busting in Rio Grande.

4   Calf roping at the annual
    Cold Lake Rodeo.

5   Rodeo clowns at The Calgary
    Stampede.

6   99th annual Millarville races.

7   Some urban rodeo action raising
    money for the local women's
    shelter, Rocky Mountain House.

8   Outriders, Strathmore.

1

2

3

4

5

6

1   Nanton All Girls Rodeo.

2   Bronco riding at the annual
    Cold Lake Rodeo.

3   Calgary Stampede Rodeo.

4   Mini-chucks, Strathmore.

5   Equestrian Ride at Lac La Biche
    horse show.

6   Rather muddy at the annual
    All Girl's Rodeo in Nanton.

7   Horse tricks, Czar.

8   Riding horse down country
    road near Rivercourse.

9   Down at the dock, Beaverdam.

10 Nanton All Girls Rodeo.

11 4-H Horse Show, Cadogan.

12 Girls on horseback,
    Cold Lake Rodeo.

13 (next spread / left) Camping in
    Dinosaur Provincial Park.

14 (next spread / upper right)
    Camping on the banks of
    Peace River.

15 (next spread / lower right)
    Girl with cat camping at Beaver
    Lake Powwow.

1   Wayne campground.

2   Fishing from the Grouard Bridge, near Grouard.

3   Camping on the banks of the Rio Grande.

4   Ice fishing, Ma-Me-O Beach.

5   Fishing from the back of the truck at Canyon Creek, Slave Lake.

6   Measuring the fish at the 10th annual Ice Fishing Derby that travels four provinces, here at Pigeon Lake.

7   Fisherman coming in from fishing on Lake Athabasca.

8   Napping at the annual Ma-Me-O Beach Ice Fishing Derby.

9   Winner (right with thumbs up) takes home 20 thousand dollars – cash – at the Pigeon Lake Ice Fishing Derby.

10 Fisherman's catch, Fort Chipewyan.

11 Fishin' from the truck. "I've fished from the back of the truck hundreds of times", Kakut Lake.

12 Gutting fish at Canyon Creek, Slave Lake.

13 Preparing the grill, Longview area.

14 (next spread) Fort Chipewyan beach.

7

8

9

10

11

12

13

1   Boating on the Peace River.

2   Sightseers on Waterton Lake.

3   Sail boat race on Cold Lake.

4   Family evening boat ride, Slave Lake.

5   The winner of the 2004 jet boat
    race on the Peace River.

6   Boater, Cold Lake.

7   Canoeing on the Bow River.

1   Dragon Boat Race with
      Edmonton skyline.

2   Paddle wheel boat on the
      Athabasca River, Athabasca.

3   Kids goofing around in
      Buffalo Lake.

4   Floating on the Elbow River.

5   Raft ride on creek near
      High Prairie.

6   Swimming in Slave Lake, Joussard.

7   Jumping into the Athabasca River,
      Fort MacKay.

8   Indoor wave pool at the West
      Edmonton Mall; surf while you shop.

9   Going for a dip at the annual
      Sunshine Splash, Sunshine Village.

10   Wading in Drumheller.

6

7

8

9

10

1

2

3

4

5

6

1   Tourists taking in the views at
    Banff Provincial Park.

2   Morning walk in coulees
    in Lethbridge.

3   Backpackers in Waterton
    National Park.

4   Ice Cave, Kananaskis Provincial Park.

5   Walking near the banks of the
    Bow River.

6   Hikers overlooking Wayne .

7   (opposite page) Hikers in
    Horseshoe Canyon.

8   (next spread) Bird counters at the
    annual spring Bird Count in the
    Cypress Hills Provincial Park.

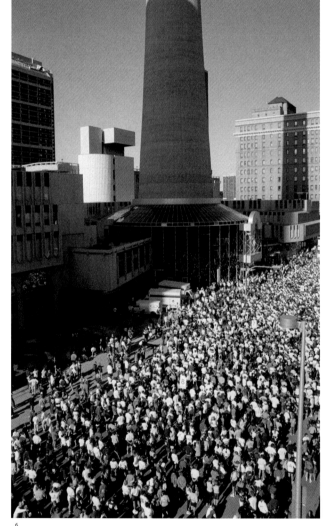

1   Cyclists at Nose Hill park, Calgary.

2   Hunting duck near Patricia.

3   Cyclists having lunch on the roadside whilst heading for Ottawa, near Cluny.

4   Rock climbing at the Buddha, Kananaskis area.

5   Warming up for the BMX competition at the 2004 Alberta Summer Games, Okotoks.

6   Mother's Day race, Calgary.

7   Medal winners, Alberta Summer Games, Okotoks.

8   Soccer at the 2004 Alberta Summer Games, Okotoks.

9   Stettler football team, Stettler.

10 Men's volleyball players shake hands at the Alberta Summer Games, High River.

11 Junior High Cross-Country races, Canada Olympic Park, Calgary.

7

8

9

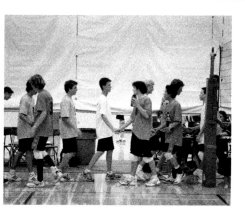

10

11

1 Hanging from the goal posts, St. Paul.

2 Babies in Team Canada hockey shirts, Edmonton.

3 Future hockey player, Lac La Biche.

4 Road hockey during Flames madness, Red Deer.

5 Road hockey on a Friday night, Kitscoty.

6 Hockey handshake at the Lac La Biche Pond Hockey tournament.

7 Athletes cheer on fellow teammates at the 2004 Alberta Summer games, Okotoks.

8 Watching Calgary Flames in the Stanley Cup playoffs.

9 Skater, La Crete.

10 The last Trappers game ever was rained out! Edmonton.

11 Baseball game in Okotoks.

12 Flames fans, Calgary.

8

9

11

12

10

1

2

3

4

1   Ice climbing competition, Nordegg.

2   200km speed skating race,
    Sylvan Lake.

3   Winning Alberta dog sled team
    at the 2004 Arctic Winter Games
    in Fort McMurray.

4   Sylvan Lake speed skating winners.

5   Snowboarders in the
    Canadian Rockies.

6   Annual New Year's Day family
    curling match, Crimson Lake.

7   Ski much?

8   Downhill skiing at Sunshine.

9   (opposite page) Alberta dog sled
    team for the Arctic Winter Games.

5

6

7

8

1   Soap Box Derby, Blackfalds.

2   Skidoo racing crowd at the
    Reynolds Museum Snow Drags.

3   Women's national body building
    winner, Edmonton.

4   Arctic Winter Games in
    Fort McMurray.

5   Hot Air Ballon, Calgary.

6   50th annual CTS racing in Red Deer.

7   Race.

8   First skidoo ride, Lac La Biche.

9   Tug-of-war at the 18th Annual Harley Davidson Appreciation Days, Wayne.

10   Truckin' in Glendon Mud Bog.

11   Cheemo Club carpet bowling champions, Blackfalds.

12   Marwayne Mud Bog.

2

3

4

6

5

7

8

1   (opposite page) Theatre dance
    troop at the annual North Country
    Fair, Jouassard.

2   The Last Oldtimers dance,
    a 23 year tradition in Eskine.

3   Yoga class in Calgary.

4   Dancing at the South Country Fair,
    Fort Macleod.

5   Drummers and Judges for
    the traditional Hand Games
    at the Arctic Winter Games,
    Fort McMurray.

6   Hoola hooping at the North
    Country Fair, Joussard.

7   Ukranian dancers at the Ukrainian
    Heritage Cultural Village.

8   Two-steppin' in Red Deer.

9   (next spread) Grand entry,
    Beaver Lake Powwow.

1   Pow Wow, Beaver Lake.

2   Scraping hide in preparation for the Beaver Lake Powwow.

3   Native dancer, Red Deer.

4   Beaver Lake Powwow.

5   Performing at the North Country Fair, Joussard.

6   Chiefs entering Powwow at Beaver Lake annual Powwow.

7   Drumming, Beaver Lake.

8   Head-Smashed-In Buffalo Jump, National Aboriginal Day.

9   Opening Ceremonies, Alberta Summer Games, High River.

10   Dancer ready for Grand Entry, Beaver Lake.

11   National Aboriginal Day, Head-Smashed-In Buffalo Jump.

8

7

9

10

11

1 (opposite page / top) Accordion
  player at the Oldtimers Dance
  at Erskine.

2 (opposite page / bottom)
  Soloist at Guitarfest, Hotchkiss.

3 Performing in Longview.

4 Texicanna Rose playing at the
  Falher Old Time Music Festival.

5 Practising Fiddle, Falher Old
  Time Music Festival.

6 Music concert, Red Deer.

7 Corb Lund in Manyberries.

8 Band practice, Calgary Stampede.

1 Music at the lift, Sunshine Village.

2 Trumpet player at Edmonton's
100th birthday party, Sir Winston
Churchill Square.

3 Tomko, Calgary.

4 Firehall fundraiser, Longview.

5 CKUA CD library, Edmonton.

6 Playing at the North Country
Fair, Slave Lake.

7 Posterboard, Calgary.

8 One Man Band, East Coulee.

9 Kids playing at the
Red Deer farmer's market.

8 Kiss tribute concert, Red Deer.

5

6

7

8

9

10

1   (opposite page) Museum
    volunteer, Strome.

2   Calgary Cares AIDS Benefit
    Fashion Show.

3   Entertainment on the Stettler
    Steam Train.

4   Art Auction, Red Deer.

5   Fashion show at the Alberta
    College of Art and Design, Calgary.

6   Art Exhibition, Calgary.

7   Onlookers scrutinize artwork
    in the park, Edmonton

1   Moving from the old museum
    to the new museum, Mallaig.

2   Indoor bull riding at Kickers
    Cookhouse Saloon, Red Deer.

3   A family poses by a helicopter at
    the Red Deer Air Show.

4   Bingo!

5   Ukrainian Heritage and
    Cultural Village.

6   Picnicking at Torrigton
    campground.

7   Alberta beef.

8   View of the North Saskatchewan
    River valley from Hotel
    MacDonald, Edmonton.

9   People G-sailing in Athabasca.

10 A young girl has her head shaved
    to raise money for cancer
    research, Red Deer.

IF IT AIN'T ALBERTA, IT AIN'T BEEF.

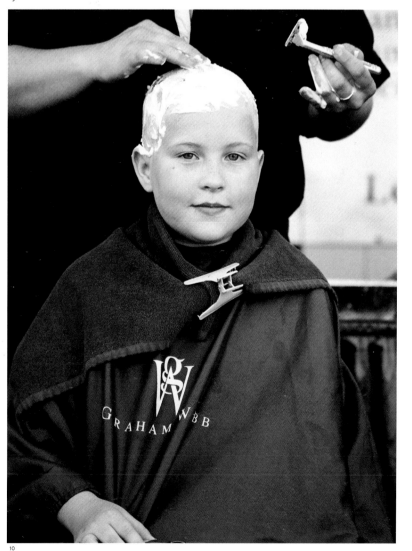

1　Food Bank donations at a
　All-Alberta-Beef barbeque,
　Red Deer.

2　Landfill rules, Fort Macleod.

3　Dumpster-diving !

4　(opposite page) Landfill.

5　(next spread) Park in Medicine Hat.

1   Boardwalk over wetlands,
    Mclennan.

2   Foothill in the Longview area.

3   Bike riding near Cluny.

4   Writing-on-stone Provincial Park.

5   Winter picnic on the rocks,
    near Nordegg.

6   Banff Hot Springs.

7   Red Deer River Valley,
    near Empress.

1   Mailboxes near Penhold.

2   Pastureland near Rockyford.

3   Transcanada Highway, Banff Exit.

4   Harvest moon 2004
    near Longview.

5   Foothills.

6   Prairie sky with farm house,
    Rockyford.

7   (opposite page) Passenger
    CP Train, eastbound between
    Canmore and Calgary.

2

3

4

5

6

7

8

1   (opposite page) Flying a kite
    overlooking the Old Man Resevoir.

2   Riding near Czar.

3   Fishing for trout at Kakut Lake.

4   Cross-country skiing on
    Lake Louise.

5   Reflecting in the Badlands, Wayne.

6   Viewing the valley on
    Waterton Lake.

7   Morning run on beach, Slave Lake.

8   Reading the newspaper in a
    park after work, Calgary.

1

2

3

4

5

1   Senior's home, Red Deer.

2   Reading at The Planet Café,
    Calgary.

3   Visiting a grave of a
    loved one, Airdrie.

4   Reading.

5   Moody windmill.

6   Hiking in the Benchlands outside
    of Canmore.

7   Biking in the Badlands.

8   Cross-country skiing, Sylvan Lake.

9   Ice surfing on Ghost Lake.

10 Pondering life on Waterton Lake.

6

8

9

7

10

1   (opposite page) New Years
    Day walk, Lake Minnewanka.

2   First solo skate, Calgary.

3   Arctic Winter Games,
    Fort McMurray.

4   Sleigh ride, Lacombe.

5   Sliding in Red Deer.

6   Pay per view, Lake Louise.

7   Father with children building
    an igloo, Didsbury.

8   Building a snow fort,
    Fort McMurray.

1   Ice skating in Ponoka.

2   Reynolds Museum, Wainwright.

3   Plowing snow, Red Deer.

4   Cropping wood, Red Deer.

5   Clearing the roads, Calgary.

6   Snow shoveling crew, Red Deer.

7   Skidoo Snow Drag Races
     at Lac La Biche.

8   Shoveling snow, Calgary.

9   Tobagganing in Calgary

5

6

7

8

9

1   (opposite page) Milk River
    character walking her dog,
    Milk River.

2   Life-long resident of Blairmore.

3   Picking Saskatoon berries,
    Meandering River.

4   St. Patrick's Day parade,
    Edmonton.

5   Tree huggers, Canmore.

6   Rodeo competitor at the Calgary
    Stampede infield.

7   Arrowheads, spearheads and
    scrappers collected over a 70
    year period.

1

2

5

3

6

4

7

8

10

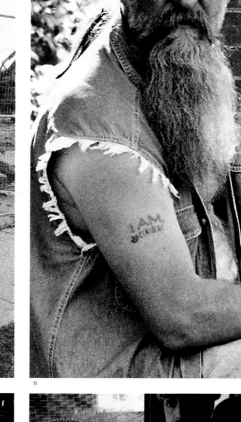

11

9

12

13

| 1 | Son of a rail-man, Carbon. | 7 | Provost boys hanging out on a hot summer's day. |

1   Son of a rail-man, Carbon.

2   Chair of the Board and entertainer / volunteer on the Stettler Steam Train.

3   Flames fan, Red Mile.

4   Picking mushrooms in field near Warburg.

5   Part-time worker at a day care.

6   The sun sets on old-timers at Hotchkiss Guitarfest.

7   Provost boys hanging out on a hot summer's day.

8   Canada Day Parade, Grande Prairie.

9   Alberta's 50th celebration signage, Innisfree.

10   Caregiver, Calgary

11   I am Canadian in Wayne.

12   Red Mile.

13   Character in Calgary.

1   Main Street, Pincher Creek.

2   Teepee and personal audio studio,
    Fort MacKay.

3   Protesting the Iraq War.

4   Afternoon walk in the town
    of Mirrow.

5   Red Mile.

6   An Alberta 75th Monument,
    Daysland.

7   (opposite page) Wagon wheel
    from 1923 journey from Montana
    to McLennan.

8   (next spread) Walking in cemetery,
    Morinville.

1   Lone cross, Manyberries.

2   Sister in Star.

3   Father greeting parish member, Star.

4   Canmore Pioneer Cemetery.

5   Father blessing cross, Mundare.

6   Canmore.

7   Funeral gathering, Morinville.

8   Cemetery, Gleichen.

9   Priest, McLennan.

10   New church, Didsbury.

11   Procession begins, Star.

12   Parish in Czar.

13   Sitting in the afternoon sun on the church steps in Smith.

14   Frog Lake Massacre.

7

8

9

10

11

12

13

14

1   (opposite page) Moment of silence
    at Remembrance Day ceremony,
    Calgary.

2   Veterans Float, Canada Day,
    Grand Prairie.

3   Veterans and some young cadets
    await Her Majesty Queen Elizabeth II
    during her walkabout in the
    Legislature Gardens, Edmonton.

4   60th D-Day events, Turner Valley.

5   D-Day commemorative events
    in Turner Valley.

6   Street sign, Exshaw.

7   Legionaires from the
    Crowsnest Pass.

8   (next spread) Newlyweds in front
    of their Bonnyville home.

1

2

3

4

1 Reminiscing the days gone by, Wetaskwin.

2 We love seniors sign, Hythe.

3 Quilting at The Ukrainian Cultural Heritage Village.

4 Supplied by the UFA, Beiseker.

5 Friends visit the Calgary Stampede.

6 46 years - combined time at the Valleyview Farmers Market.

7 Longtime friends near Spirit River.

8 Oldtimers watch as a long time friend's farm gets auctioned off, Fort Kent.

9 Alberta Senior's Men's Horse Shoe Champions at tournament in Lac La Biche.

5

6

8

7

9

1 (opposite page) Happy as could be after 52 years of marriage, McLennan.

2 Couple by teepee, Beaver Lake Reserve.

3 Couple taking a walk to the coffee shop in Cereal.

4 Couple enjoying the peace and quiet of their own backyard, McLennan.

5 Newlyweds at the McDougall Church near Morley.

6 Couple planting garden near Mundare.

7 Couple having a quiet moment near the banks of the Glenmore reservoir, Calgary.

1   Cowboy couple, Czar.

2   Residents of the Manyberries'
    train station.

3   Happily married Hutterite couple
    selling produce at the Viking
    farmers market.

4   Couple walking near Andrew.

5   (opposite page) Couple at the
    North Country Fair, Joussard.

6   (next spread) Mother and daughter
    reading books on the banks of
    Slave Lake.

1   Mother with new born, Czar.

2   First boat ride for the little one, on the Peace River.

3   Two friends sitting in the shade, Assumption.

4   James and darling daughter Lilly at the fair, Red Deer.

5   Horsing around down at the dock on a Friday night, Slave Lake.

6   Brother and sister working in the beet patch of their family u-pick-it business, Smokey Lake.

7   Family portrait, Cluny Colony.

8   Family tobogganing in Red Deer.

9   Brother and sister at the Stampede Parade.

10   Mother and son funny-car racing team near Leduc.

11   Mennonite family picking strawberries near Peace River.

12   Mom with her two girls.

13   Proud father with new-born baby.

14   Ukranian New Year's dinner, Red Deer.

8

9

10

11

12

13

14

1   Brothers stand before the homestead house their parents built, back when they were small boys, Wainwright area.

2   Friends skateboarding down Main Street Bashaw.

3   Brothers skating on a frozen puddle in Harvie Heights, just outside of Canmore.

4   North Country Fair, Slave Lake.

5   Brothers and sons help their elder in Star.

6   (opposite page) Brothers delivering newspapers with wagon, Red Deer.

7   (next spread / left) Leading her horse after competition at the Nanton All Girls Rodeo.

8   (next spread / left) Young boys on the Assumption Reserve.

1   No Adults, Lac La Biche.

2   Shoveling snow for the first time,
    Fort McMurray.

3   Inspecting an old tree
    in Athabasca.

4   Having some ice cream in Eztikom.

5   Kids riding the train at Heritage
    Park, Calgary.

6   Red Deer skateboarding park.

7   King of the sand castle, Slave Lake.

8   Boy Scouts in High River.

9   Fishing for minnows, Crimson Lake.

10 Small boy getting a drink on a
    very hot day, Wayne.

11 At the All Girls Rodeo in Nanton.

12 Kids cooling off with a cold drink,
    Red Deer.

7

8

9

10

11

12

1   Three-legged race.

2   Kids playing cap guns at the
    4H Rodeo, Czar.

3   Riding the merry-go-round
    in Calgary.

4   Kids enjoying the playground,
    Calgary.

5   Daughter of the book designer,
    Calgary.

6   (opposite page) Kids sliding at
    the Calgary Stampede.

1   Watching the demise of the local grain elevator, Beiseker.

2   Friendship circle at Head-Smashed-In Buffalo Jump Interpretive Centre.

3   Singing at the Opening Ceremonies of the Alberta Summer Games, High River.

4   Back to school photo in Red Deer.

5   Kids on dock, Kakut Lake.

6   Girl taking in the Canada Day Celebrations in Banff.

7   Doubling down Main Street Bashaw.

8   (opposite page) I Am Albertan.

This Country Canada

This Country Canada Ltd. (TCC) is a non-profit company devoted to the discovery and documentation of Canada and Canadians. Co-directed by Kristen Wagner and Tim Van Horn, TCC has a passion for preserving the true-life stories of ordinary Canadians in the belief that they are an essential part of our unfolding history. Through the use of photography, audio recording, and video, as well as by gathering artifacts, the company is building the archives of the future. At the same time, the work is brought to the contemporary public through exhibitions, media articles, audio visual presentations and books.

The I Am Albertan Project

TCC is celebrating the once-in-a-lifetime milestone of Alberta's first centennial with one of the most extensive documentations of the province ever undertaken. For three years, between 2002 and early 2005, Kristen Wagner and Tim Van Horn traveled thousands of kilometers, met thousands of people, and shot a thousand rolls of film. Driving from north to south, and east to west, they discovered, as they had always suspected, that Alberta's greatest resource is the strong, unsung and eclectic mix of people who call this place home.

TCC was disappointed that the Alberta Government's Centennial Committee chose not to provide any funding for celebratory projects or publications. As a result, raising funds for *I Am Albertan* was an uphill struggle. Nonetheless, with typical Alberta grit, Kristen and Tim proceeded with *I Am Albertan*, determined to create a fitting tribute for the province's first centennial. They kept expenses to a minimum by sleeping in their vans and eating lots of bread and cheese. Albertans across the province let the photographers camp in their yards and invited them in for supper; generosity that was gratefully received.

As they documented the province, Kristen and Tim sought to discover what it is that makes people distinctly Albertan. Through their travels, they began to realize that there was no succinct description for Albertans. The more they tried to define Albertans, the more elusive the definition became. As they traveled, they met people from all over the world, each with their own expectations and dreams; some had come from elsewhere, some were born in Alberta, all had chosen to live their lives here. Instead of forcing the province to fit into a stereotype, Kristen and Tim decided the best representation of Alberta would be found in a diverse array of images.

I Am Albertan contains photos from every corner of the province; from the Premier to the factory worker, there are Albertans at work, at play, in solitude, at social gatherings and at home. From the top of the province to the bottom, *I Am Albertan* invites you to find yourself on the pages of this legacy book. A story about the people, for the people, I Am Albertan is a vibrant look at who we are after 100 years as a province.

Kristen Wagner

Kristen is a native of Calgary. As a kid, she went to a Liberal Party rally with a newly broken arm and presented her cast to Prime Minister Pierre Trudeau for him to sign. It was 1973 and Ottawa and Alberta had just started fighting over oil. A week later, when Premier Peter Lougheed visited her school, Kristen asked him to sign her cast too. As Lougheed looked for a space on the cast, he saw Trudeau's name. The Premier looked at Kristen for a moment, then laughed and signed his name alongside the Prime Minister's.

When she grew up, Kristen studied film and photography at Ryerson Polytechnical Institute, than worked in West Germany for eight years doing photography, animation and special effects for documentary films. Her passion for innovative presentation of educational subject matter, and a vision that moves her to document ordinary Canadian life in extraordinary ways, led to Kristen's involvement in founding This Country Canada.

The I Am Albertan project was a perfect opportunity for Kristen to put her vision and passion for documentary into play. She welcomed the chance to meet Albertans across the province and came home with many good memories and only one bad scare that happened while camping in her van in a prairie town. The frantic barking of her dog Billy woke Kristen twice that night as vandals prepared to smash her windows. For weeks afterwards, Billy would spend the night watching from the front seat of the van, refusing to got to bed.

Kristen's favorite I Am Albertan shoot took place on a rainy spring day in the Cypress Hills where she tagged along with a group of birders. She was amazed by the knowledge of the birders, especially a Medicine Hat high school science teacher who had begun birding with his grandmother when he was three years old. Kristen surprised herself and the group when she was the one to spot a brown creeper, a small nuthatch-like bird that had never been seen before in the Cypress Hills. The group identified over 60 birds that day.

Kristen lives in Okotoks with her three wonderful daughters and Billy the dog.

Tim Van Horn

Tim was born in Edmonton, but with a father in the Canadian Armed Forces, he didn't stay there long. The family spent time in Bermuda and Inuvik before moving to the Queen Charlotte Islands. For Tim, the islands were a boy's paradise where he was up early to comb the beaches and explore the forests. By the time he was 10, his father was transferred to the Cold Lake base and Tim came back to Alberta where he has been ever since.

Tim made the decision to be a photographer at a young age, attracted to a profession that would allow him to continue exploring the world. A celebrated alumnus of the Alberta College of Art & Design, Tim has established himself in the Canadian photography scene where his work has appeared in numerous archives, private collections, magazines, newspapers, and travelling exhibitions. A co-founder of This Country Canada, Tim carries his camera daily, documenting the lives of Canadians from all walks of life wherever they may be.

On the I Am Albertan project, Tim logged thousands of miles and saw much of the province, making it all the way to the northern border with the Northwest Territories. During his travels, Tim had a close call with a bull, received stitches for a dog bite, got hung up on a tall fence, and was almost run over by a grain auger when a farmer ran a stop sign. His worst shoot was with honey collectors in Thiesen near Bonneyville where he was stung 10 times on the nose, neck and chin. Despite the mishaps, Tim had a fabulous time exploring Alberta. His most exhilarating morning on the road was spent in a helicopter flying over a forest near Whitecourt on the way to a tree planting block. The chopper pilot flew low to the ground, skimming hills and banking over trees while Tim hung out the door taking photographs.

Tim lives in Red Deer with his dogs Bo and Maya.

CONTRIBUTORS

Brock Silversides

An archivist with a passion for photography, Brock is the author of 10 books and exhibition catalogues and over 50 articles related to Canadian photography and film. Born in Ottawa, he grew up in Saskatoon where he received a degree in history before studying library science at the University of Western Ontario.

Over the years, Brock has worked for the Saskatoon Public Library, the National Library of Canada, the Saskatchewan Archives Board, the Medicine Hat Museum & Art Gallery, and spent 10 years as the Chief Audio-Visual Archivist at the Provincial Archives of Alberta. He is currently the Director of Media Commons at the Robarts Library at the University of Toronto. What Brock misses most about the prairies is the light, the clear air, and grain elevators.

Sandra Shields

Writer Sandra Shields is a fourth generation Albertan who grew up listening to stories about how one great-grandmother spent the winter in a dugout, how another crouched in a creek to survive a prairie fire, and how her grandfather took his teacher's salary in chickens and vegetables.

The oldest of nine children, Sandra studied philosophy and political science at the University of Calgary before receiving a Masters degree from Carleton University. She works with her husband photographer David Campion. Their first book, Where Fire Speaks: A visit with the Himba, won the Hubert Evans Award. Their second book, The Company of Others: Stories of Belonging, documents circles of friends formed around people with disabilities.

Combine Design & Communications

Combine is an award-winning Calgary design studio co-founded by Dean Bartsch and Dwayne Dobson. With everyone in the company hailing from the West, Combine is proud of its prairie roots. Because of a strong belief in the work of artists in Alberta and across the West, the company has focused on collaborating with local talent to help establish a strong voice for Western Canadian arts and culture.

BIBLIOGRAPHY

About the photographs

The photographs in this book were made by Kristen Wagner and Tim Van Horn between 2002 and 2005, with the exception of several photos taken by Peter Manolakas. Mike Drew took the photo of Kristen and Tim with the Alberta sign.

Photos from the Glenbow Archive in the Then & Now section include:
na-184-63, na-544-66, na-559-11, na-670-65, na-945-4, na-1237-6, na-1263-8, na-1297-4, na-1586-22, na-1824-1, na-2194-4, na-2804-1, na-3051-5, na-3146-2, na-3474-8, na-3874-1, nb-16-621, nd-3-6742, nd-8-219.

Sources

The information in I Am Albertan was obtained from:

Government of Alberta
Statistics Canada
Government of Canada
Calgary Public Library
Alberta Beef Producers
Canadian Association of Petroleum Producers
Growing Alberta
Participatory Democracy Group

Sources continued

Alberta Views Magazine
Canadian Geographic Magazine
Alberta: A New History by Howard Palmer
The Best Edmonton Stories by Tony Cashman
Boondoggles, Bonanzas, Other
Alberta Stories by Brian Brennan
Calgary: Spirit of the West by Hugh A. Dempsey
Grant MacEwan's West: Sketches
from the Past by Grant MacEwan
Mavericks: An Incorrigible History
of Alberta by Aritha Van Herk
The Promised Land: Settling the West
by Pierre Berton